MEXICAN
FEASTS

MEXICAN

FEASTS

50 dishes full of fire and spice

ELIZABETH LAMBERT ORTIZ

southwater

This edition is published by Southwater

Southwater is an imprint of
Anness Publishing Limited
Hermes House
88–89 Blackfriars Road
London SE1 8HA
tel. 020 7401 2077
fax 020 7633 9499

Distributed in the UK by
The Manning Partnership
251–253 London Road East
Batheaston
Bath BA1 7RL
tel. 01225 852 727
fax 01225 852 852

Distributed in the USA by
Anness Publishing Inc.
27 West 20th Street
Suite 504
New York
NY 10011
tel. 212 807 6739
fax 212 807 6813

Distributed in Australia by
Sandstone Publishing
Unit 1
360 Norton Street
Leichhardt
New South Wales 2040
tel. 02 9560 7888
fax 02 9560 7488

1 3 5 7 9 10 8 6 4 2

Publisher: Joanna Lorenz
Project editor: Joanne Rippin
Designer: Ian Sandom
Production Controller: Joanna King
Editorial Reader: Marion Wilson
Photography: David Jordan

Additional photographs by: William Adams-Lingwood, Steve Baxter,
James Duncan and Thomas Odulate

For all recipes, quantities are given in both metric and imperial
measures, and, where appropriate, measures are also given in standard
cups and spoons. Follow one set, but not a mixture, because they are
not interchangeable.

Previously published as Best-ever Mexican Cookbook

CONTENTS

INTRODUCTION

There's no longer any need to travel far to enjoy marvellous Mexican food. Mexican restaurants are springing up all over the place, and Mexican ingredients like chillies, tortillas and refried beans are hot favourites, available in supermarkets and even small grocery stores.

Much of what most of us think of as Mexican cooking is actually Tex-Mex. Texas was once part of Mexico, and Texans retain a love of the spicy flavours that characterize that country's cuisine. Americans adopted – and adapted – traditional Mexican recipes and the result is a blend that has become a style of cooking in its own right. Tex-Mex food is popular the world over, and some of it is very good indeed, but while it has strong echoes of its origins, it isn't entirely authentic.

To taste true Mexican cooking you need to seek out specialist restaurants rather than fast-food outlets, and experiment with recipes like those in this collection, which are a genuine celebration of Mexican cuisine. Little-known dishes like Salt Cod in Mild Chilli Sauce or Seviche or Beef with Cactus Pieces are excellent examples, as are Chilaquiles, Crab with Green Rice and Chayote Salad. No collection of Mexican recipes would be complete without Mole Poblano de Guajolote, an intriguing combination of turkey, chillies and chocolate. Though this may sound extraordinary, you have only to taste it to understand why it is first choice for Mexican festivals and family celebrations.

More familiar favourites like Enchiladas, Quesadillas, Chimichangas and meltingly sweet Churros complete this lingering look at Mexican cooking, and the book concludes with a chapter on drinks, from devilish Tequila Cocktail to soothing Mexican Hot Chocolate.

A comprehensive guide to ingredients describes *pepitas*, *piloncillo* and tomatillos and their uses, and suggests substitutes for foodstuffs that haven't yet found their way on to our supermarket shelves. This indispensable guide to Mexican cooking makes all its vibrant flavours accessible and irresistible.

Storecupboard Ingredients

A well-stocked storecupboard makes sense when it comes to Mexican cooking. Everyday ingredients like dried beans and chick-peas keep extremely well, and form the basis of a wide range of tasty dishes. Less familiar items may require a visit to a specialist food store, so it makes sense to lay in supplies when the opportunity presents itself.

Achiote (Annatto)
Prized for its flavouring and colouring qualities, this comes from the hard, orange-red coating around the seeds of a tropical American flowering tree, *Bixa orellana*. The pulp, dissolved in oil or water, imparts a delicate flavour and a deep, golden-orange colour. The small seeds are used whole or ground as a flavouring.

Almonds
Both whole and ground almonds are used in sweet and savoury dishes; ground almonds are an important ingredient in Mole Poblano de Guajolote.

Beans (dried)
Dried beans (*frijoles*) are a staple in the Mexican diet, either served with a little of the cooking liquid, or mashed and fried with lard as refritos. Pink, red and black haricot beans are native to Mexico, as are speckled pinto beans. Also popular are lima beans from Peru, red kidney beans and chick-peas (*garbanzos*). Canned beans are a useful stand-by, as are cans of refried beans.

Capers
Capers are a popular Mexican flavouring. Buy them in jars and store them in the fridge after opening.

Chocolate
Chocolate originated in Mexico thousands of years ago. Mexican chocolate is flavoured with cinnamon, almonds and vanilla. It is sold in blocks for use in drinks and cooking. If you cannot locate it, use any bitter chocolate that is high in cocoa solids.

Chorizo
This highly seasoned sausage, popular in Spain and Mexico, comes in many varieties, but all contain pork and paprika.

Masa harina
Dried maize kernels are ground to make *masa harina*, the flour which is used to make tortillas, tamales and other baked goods. *Masa harina* is also used to thicken a hot chocolate drink.

Nopales/Nopalitos
The paddles of the prickly pear cactus, these are sold fresh in Mexican markets. We must make do with canned *nopales*. Look for them in specialist food stores.

Pepitas
These small, plump pumpkin seeds are very popular in Mexico, and are used whole or ground. Regular hulled pumpkin seeds of the sort that are sold in health food shops can be used instead.

Pickled jalapeño chillies
Full of flavour and not too hot, these are very useful. Buy them in jars or cans. You can also buy plain *jalapeños* in cans.

Piloncillo
This is an unrefined dark brown cane sugar, sold in cone-shaped loaves in Mexico. It tastes like molasses and is used to sweeten desserts and coffee. Soft dark brown sugar is a good substitute for *piloncillo*.

Spices
Chillies are the principal Mexican spice, but ground cumin and ground coriander are also used. Cinnamon is a popular ingredient in savoury dishes, both in the stick and ground, while peppercorns and cloves feature in many recipes. Herbs are generally used fresh in Mexican dishes, but some recipes include dried oregano and bay leaves.

Sweetcorn kernels
There are many different varieties of corn in Mexico, and the fresh kernels are widely used. Cans of whole-kernel corn are a useful storecupboard item for those occasions when fresh corn is not available. Look for canned sweetcorn which does not have added salt or sugar.

Tomatillos
In Mexico these fruits are used fresh, but at present you will probably only be able to find them in 275 g/10 oz cans. Tomatillos are sometimes called Mexican green tomatoes, but are actually related to physalis and not to tomatoes. They have an exquisite flavour.

Tortillas
Tortillas are round, thin pancakes made from masa harina or wheat flour. The dough is pressed flat in a wooden tortilla press then cooked on a griddle. Mexican cooks make their own each day or buy them freshly made from tortillerias; you can make them yourself or buy flour tortillas in vacuum packs. Provided the pack is securely sealed, these keep well and are very useful for impromptu meals.

Vermicelli
Pasta is not widely used in Mexican cooking, but vermicelli is a popular addition to soup.

OPPOSITE (CLOCKWISE FROM TOP LEFT): Pepitas *(pumpkin seeds), star anise,* masa harina, *plain flour, cinnamon sticks, Mexican chocolate and almonds.*

Fresh Produce

Mexican markets are ablaze with colour. Chillies of every size and hue, sweet peppers, fat red tomatoes, acid green limes and oranges are just a few of the colourful vegetables and fruits that are piled high on the stalls. Although the range may not be as extensive, you should be able to buy most of the fresh ingredients needed for authentic Mexican dishes in your local supermarket.

OPPOSITE (CLOCKWISE FROM TOP LEFT): *Avocados, string of garlic, chayotes, garlic bulb, tomatoes, onions, canned tomatillos and* jalapeño *chillies (in bowl), courgettes, lemons and lime halves (centre).*

Avocados

Although the avocado is now grown all over the world, it originated in Central America. There are nearly five hundred varieties but only three distinct types. The Mexican avocado is a small fruit with a thin skin, anise-scented leaves and a high oil content. The most famous avocado dish is guacamole, which is served with tortilla dishes, refried beans and as a dip.

Bananas

Grown in all tropical parts of Mexico which have sufficient rainfall, bananas are an important food source. There are several different varieties, including red-skinned bananas, which are sometimes eaten raw in Mexico but more often cooked. Plantains, which are related to bananas, must be cooked. Their flesh is not always sweet.

Chayotes

Pear-shaped or round, these squash are indigenous to Mexico but are now widely exported. Also known as christophines or *chochos*, they have a firm, crisp flesh and a large, delicate seed. Chayotes have a mild flavour and are a popular addition to salads and soups.

Coconuts

Both green and ripe coconuts are widely used in all Central and South American countries. Freshly grated coconut is used in savoury and sweet dishes, and is the prime ingredient in a delicious custard pudding.

Courgettes

Courgettes and other summer squash are popular Mexican vegetables, and are often combined with tomatoes and chillies. The flowers are used as well as the courgettes themselves: if you grow courgettes, harvest the male flowers for cooking so that your vegetable crop is not diminished.

Garlic

This universal flavouring is as popular in Mexico as it is elsewhere. Introduced to the New World by the Spanish, garlic was enthusiastically adopted and appears in many Mexican dishes.

Limes, Lemons and Oranges

These citrus fruits are grown in the tropical regions of Mexico, along the coasts, and are full of flavour. Mexican oranges tend to be quite pale in colour, but are very sweet.

Onions

Like garlic, onions were introduced by the Spanish and are now very widely used.

Papayas

The papayas sold in Mexico are large fruit, often providing up to ten servings. The flesh is bright orange or yellow and has a superb flavour which is delicious on its own or with a squeeze of lime juice.

Tomatillos

These tasty fruits are related to physalis. Fresh tomatillos are seldom available outside their countries of origin, but can be bought in cans (see Storecupboard Ingredients).

Tomatoes

Fat beefsteak tomatoes and juicy plum tomatoes are important ingredients in Mexican cooking. Use sun-ripened vine fruit where possible. In winter, when tomatoes tend to lack flavour, it is better to substitute canned tomatoes.

Chillies and Peppers

Chillies and sweet peppers are such fundamental flavourings in Mexican cooking that they deserve special mention. There are well over a hundred different varieties of chilli in Mexico, with varying degrees of heat, from mildly warming to pure dynamite. Sweet peppers, sometimes called bell peppers, are not hot at all. In the list below, where chillies and peppers are rated from zero to ten in terms of their heat, peppers score the lowest possible mark. You may not be able to find all these varieties locally, although the range is improving. Dried chillies are easier to come by, and some specialist importers sell them by mail order.

OPPOSITE (CLOCKWISE FROM TOP LEFT): *Small green chillies,* chipotle *chillies,* mulato *chillies,* habanero *chillies,* pasilla *chillies, green peppers, green* jalapeño *chillies and* anaheim *chillies. The red chillies in the centre are* Habanero *or Scotch Bonnets (left) and* serranos *(right).*

Anaheim chillies
These long, tapered chillies, sometimes known as long green chillies, are widely available. They are sweet and mild, with a heatscale rating of 2-3.

Ancho chillies
Anchos are dried *poblano* chillies. They are sweet, fruity and mild, with a heatscale rating of 3. They need to be soaked in warm water to soften them before use, and as with many varieties of chilli, an initial roasting or grilling enhances their flavour. *Anchos* are often stuffed, cut into strips or added to *mole* sauces.

Chipotle chillies
These are simply smoked *jalapeños*. They have a nutty, smoky flavour and are fairly hot, with a heatscale rating of 6.

Guajillo chillies
Said to taste like green tea, *guajillos* are relatively mild, with a heatscale rating of 3. They are used in many classic *salsas*.

Jalapeño chillies
These are the most widely available of all the chilli varieties. Usually sold when they are a clear apple green colour, *jalapeños* are moderately hot, scoring 5-6 on the heatscale. In Mexico, some *jalapeños* are left on the bush to ripen to a clear, bright red. Both plain and pickled *jalapeños* are also available in cans and jars. Smoked *jalapeños* are known as *chipotles*.

Mulato chillies
Tasting of a mixture of aniseed, tobacco and cherry, these are dried chillies. They have a heatscale rating of 3 and are sold in various grades, depending on quality and flavour.

Pasilla chillies
Ranging from dark brown through purple to black, these dark, wrinkled chillies have a heatscale rating of 4. Ground *pasillas* are often used in commercially prepared chilli powders and pastes.

Poblano chillies
These green or red chillies are usually roasted and peeled before being used. They are highly valued in Mexico for their delicious earthy, chocolatey flavour rather than their fire. With a heatscale rating of only 3, they are often mixed with hotter chillies in slow-cooked stews and wonderful, complex sauces. When dried, they are known as *ancho* chillies.

Habanero or Scotch Bonnet chillies
The name describes these chunky little chillies perfectly. Related to *habaneros*, they are also fiercely hot, with the maximum heatscale rating of 10. They are fairly widely available fresh.

Serrano chillies
These plump chillies can be green or red, and have a clean, sharp flavour. Hotter than *jalapeños*, they have a heatscale rating of 7. *Serranos* are often used in guacamole.

Sweet peppers
These bell-shaped peppers are available in a range of colours - green, yellow, orange, red and black. They are popular the world over, in salads, *salsas* and baked dishes. Whole or half peppers are often stuffed. Roasting intensifies their mild flavour. Their heatscale rating is 0.

Chilli Flowers
Use mild chillies to make this attractive garnish. Slit the chillies lengthways, leaving the stem ends intact, and gently scrape out any seeds. Cut lengthways into as many strips as possible. Drop the chillies into a bowl of iced water and put in the fridge for several hours until the "petals" have curled back.

TECHNIQUES

Preparing Chillies

The hottest chillies need very careful handling – just follow these simple steps. If you do touch chillies, wash your hands thoroughly.

1 To remove the skin from habanero chillies, skewer the chillies, one at a time, on a metal fork and hold over a gas flame for 2–3 minutes, turning the chilli until the skin blackens and blisters.

2 Leave the chillies to cool for a few minutes, then use a clean dish towel to rub off the skins.

3 Try not to touch the chillies with your bare hands; wear rubber gloves or use a fork to hold them and slice them open with a sharp knife.

4 Even the less hot varieties of chillies can be fairly fiery. To reduce the heat, cut the chillies in half and scrape out the seeds using the tip of a knife blade.

Peeling Peppers

Peppers are delicious added raw to salads. However, roasting them first softens the flesh and gives them a wonderfully rich flavour.

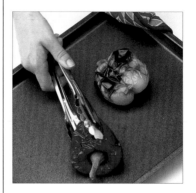

1 Preheat the grill to medium. Place the peppers on a baking sheet and grill for 8–12 minutes, turning regularly, until the skins have blackened and blistered.

2 Place the peppers in a bowl and cover with a clean dish towel. Leave for 5 minutes so the stem helps to lift the skin away from the flesh.

3 When the peppers are cool enough to handle, pierce a hole in the bottom of each one and gently squeeze out the juices into a bowl.

4 Peel off and discard the skins from the peppers and then chop or slice as required in recipes.

Chopping Onions

Uniform-sized dice make cooking easy. This method can't be beaten.

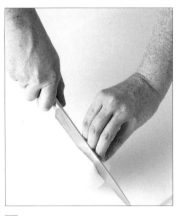

1 Peel the onion. Cut it in half with a large knife and set it cut-side down on a board. Make vertical cuts lengthways along the onion, cutting almost but not quite through to the root.

2 Make two horizontal cuts from the stalk end towards the root, but not through it.

3 Cut the onion crossways to form small, even dice.

Slicing Onions

Use thin slices for sautéing, in salsas or fish dishes like Escabeche, or use sweet onion slices in salads.

1 Peel the onion. Cut it in half with a large knife and set it cut-side down on a chopping board.

2 Cut out a triangular piece of the core from each half.

3 Cut across each half in vertical slices.

Peeling, Seeding and Chopping Tomatoes

Tomatoes feature extensively in Mexican dishes. Here is a simple and efficient way to prepare them.

Preparing Garlic

Don't worry if you don't have a garlic press: try this method, which gives wonderfully juicy results.

1 Use a sharp knife to cut a small cross on the bottom of the tomato.

2 Turn the tomato over and cut out the stem end and core.

3 Immerse the tomato in a pan of boiled water for about 10–15 seconds, then transfer to a bowl of cold water using a slotted spoon.

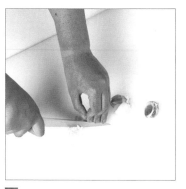

1 Break off the clove of garlic, place the flat side of a large knife on top and strike with your fist. Remove all the papery outer skin. Begin by finely chopping the clove.

4 Lift out the tomato and peel it (the skin should be easy to remove).

5 Cut the tomato in half crossways and squeeze out the seeds.

6 Use a sharp knife to cut the peeled tomato into strips, then chop across the strips to make dice.

2 Sprinkle over a little table salt and, using the flat side of a large knife blade, work the salt into the garlic, until the clove softens and releases its juices. Use as required.

Browning Meat

This is very important when making stews and casseroles: the browner the meat, the richer the colour and flavour of the dish.

Skinning Fish Fillets

Some Mexican fish dishes require skinned fish fillets. The technique is easy when you know how.

1 Heat the pan, with a little oil, until very hot. Don't add the meat when the fat is only warm or it won't seal the outside of the meat and you'll lose a lot of the meat juices.

1 Lay the fish flat on a clean board, skin-side down, with the tail towards you. Using a sharp knife with a flexible blade, make a slit between the skin and flesh of the fillet.

2 Add a few pieces of meat at a time, depending on the size of the pan, and allow them to turn a rich golden brown, turning to brown all sides. Keep the heat quite high, but take care, as the fat will spit. Don't add the meat all at once as this reduces the heat dramatically and the meat will stew instead of sealing.

3 Remove the meat with a slotted spoon to drain off as much fat as possible, and place on kitchen paper. Repeat with the remaining meat.

2 Hold the skin with one hand. Place the knife between the skin and flesh with the blade almost horizontal. Use a gentle sawing motion to remove the flesh, holding the skin taut underneath.

Peeling a Pineapple

Try this simple but effective way of removing the skin from a fresh pineapple.

1 Holding the pineapple in one hand on a chopping board, cut off the leafy top using a large, sharp knife.

2 Cutting at a 45° angle, make an incision in the pineapple skin, following the natural diagonal line of the eyes. When you reach the end of the line, turn the pineapple over and cut the other side of the line of eyes in the same way. Pull off the strip of skin.

3 Continue cutting the skin of the pineapple in the same way until it is completely peeled, then slice or chop as required in the recipe.

Preparing Mangoes

Mexicans often serve fresh fruit instead of a rich dessert. Mangoes are the perfect choice.

1 Holding the mango upright on a chopping board, use a large knife to slice the flesh away from either side of the large, flat stone in two pieces.

2 Using a smaller knife, carefully trim away the flesh still clinging to the stone. Score the flesh of the mango halves deeply, then turn the mango half round and cut lines in the opposite direction.

3 Carefully turn the skin inside out so that the flesh stands out like hedgehog spikes. Slice the diced flesh away from the skin.

Segmenting Oranges

Orange segments without any skin are useful for adding to salsas.

1 Slice the bottom off the orange so that it will stand firmly on a chopping board. Using a sharp knife, remove the peel by slicing from the top to the bottom of the orange.

2 Hold the orange in one hand over a bowl. Slice towards the middle of the fruit, to one side of the segment, and then gently twist the knife to ease the segment away from the membrane and out of the orange. Repeat to remove all of the segments. Squeeze any juice from the remaining membrane into the bowl.

Preparing Avocados

Removing the flesh from avocados is easy to do.

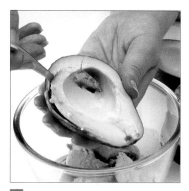

1 Cut around the avocado, twist to separate the halves, remove the stone, then scoop out the flesh into a bowl.

2 Mash the flesh well with a fork or a potato masher, or tip out on to a board and chop finely using a large knife.

Crushing Ice

Tequila cocktails are served over crushed ice. It is not a good idea to do this in a blender or food processor as you may find it makes the blade blunt.

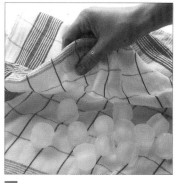

1 Lay a cloth on a work surface and cover half of the cloth with ice cubes. Alternatively, place the ice cubes in a cloth ice bag.

2 Fold the cloth over and, using the end of a rolling pin or a wooden mallet, strike the ice firmly, several times, until you achieve the required fineness.

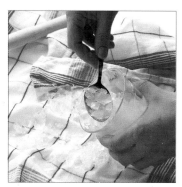

3 Spoon or scrape the fine ice snow into glasses or a jug. Fine ice snow must be used immediately, but cracked or roughly crushed ice can be stored in the freezer in plastic bags.

Planning a Mexican Meal

There are no hard-and-fast rules about planning a Mexican meal, other than to ensure that everyone has a good time. Mexicans' enjoyment of life extends to their love of good food, drink and excellent company. With those ingredients, you simply can't go wrong.

Mexicans traditionally eat four meals a day, although this pattern is changing.

Breakfast is usually substantial, with fruit and sweet breads or tortillas accompanied by coffee or chocolate. It is not unusual for meat or eggs to be served at this time.

The main meal of the day, *comida*, is a long, late lunch which starts at around 1pm. Modern Mexicans may eat relatively sparingly (and may even adopt the Western practice of eating dinner at night), but their forebears really made a feast of it. Their idea of a decent lunch was a hearty soup followed by a chicken, game or fish dish served with salads. That was just for starters – after that came the main course, which consisted of beef, lamb or pork with an array of vegetables. Just in case the diners were still not satisfied, a small dish of beans (usually red kidney or pinto) would be served, either solo or with a generous topping of cheese. Dessert today is usually fresh fruit, but in the past a baked pudding or custard was also offered. It is not difficult to see why a siesta came to be considered absolutely essential!

Merienda is an early evening meal, designed to revitalize working men and women on their return home. Traditionally it consisted of *atole* - a corn gruel – served with *tamales*, cakes, biscuits or sweet breads. This used to be followed by a sizeable late night supper, served at around 10pm, but the practice has dwindled, except on formal occasions.

Altering their pattern of eating doesn't necessarily mean that Mexicans eat less. Snacks are hugely popular, and street vendors do a brisk trade in *tamales*, tacos, sandwiches and little cakes.

If you are planning to serve a Mexican meal, much will depend on the nature of the occasion. Teenagers tramping home after a football match would enjoy Chimichangas or Red Enchiladas, perhaps served with a simple Chayote Salad. An after-theatre supper could consist of Prawns in Red Sauce on a bed of rice, followed by Caramel Custard (flan). If you want to serve a truly authentic, formal Mexican lunch, you could start with Tlalpeño-style Soup, then offer small portions of Seviche with Green Bean and Sweet Red Pepper Salad. After a main course such as Mole Poblano de Guajolote (served with rice, tortillas and guacamole) you may wish to forgo the traditional dish of beans and offer a fairly light dessert, such as Coconut Custard, or simply Almond Biscuits with coffee.

Corn Tortillas

Have ready a tortilla press and a small plastic bag,
cut open and halved crossways.

Makes about 14

INGREDIENTS
275 g/10 oz/2 cups *masa harina*
    (tortilla flour)
250–350 ml/8–12 fl oz/1–1½ cups
    water

masa harina

water

1 Put the *masa harina* into a bowl
and stir in 250 ml/8 fl oz/1 cup of the
water, mixing to a soft dough that just
holds together. If it is too dry, add a
little more water. Cover the bowl with
a cloth and set aside for 15 minutes.
Meanwhile, preheat the oven to
150°C/300°F/ Gas 2.

COOK'S TIP

It is the *masa harina* that makes corn
tortillas different to flour tortillas, and
gives a particularly Mexican flavour to
the dishes. If you can't get hold of
masa harina, make the flour tortillas
on the facing page; you can use either
kind for most Mexican recipes.

Tortillas are very easy to make but it
is important to get the dough texture
right. If it is too dry and crumbly, add
a little water; if it is too wet, add
more *masa harina*. If you misjudge
the pressure needed for flattening the
ball of dough to a neat circle on the
tortilla press, just scrape it off, roll it
back into a ball and try again.

2 Knead the dough lightly and shape
into 14 balls. Open the tortilla press and
line both sides with the prepared plastic
sheets. Put a ball on the press and bring
the top down firmly to flatten the dough
out into a round.

3 Preheat a griddle until hot. Open
the press. Peel off the top layer of
plastic and lift the tortilla by means of
the bottom plastic. Turn it on to your
palm, so that the plastic is uppermost.
Peel off the plastic and flip the tortilla on
to the hot griddle.

4 Cook for about 1 minute or until
the edges start to curl. Turn over and
cook for a further 1 minute. Wrap in foil
and keep warm in the oven while you
press and cook the remaining tortillas.

Flour Tortillas

You don't need a tortilla press to make these.
Simply roll them out.

Makes about 14

INGREDIENTS
225 g/8 oz/2 cups plain flour
5 ml/1 tsp salt
15 ml/1 tbsp lard or vegetable fat
120 ml/4 fl oz/½ cup water

flour

salt

water

lard

1 Sift the flour and salt into a mixing bowl. Rub in the lard or vegetable fat with your fingertips until the mixture resembles coarse breadcrumbs.

2 Gradually add the water and mix to a soft dough. Knead lightly, form into a ball, cover the bowl with a cloth and leave to rest for 15 minutes.

3 Divide the dough into about 14 portions and form into balls. Roll out each ball of dough in turn on a lightly floured board to a round measuring about 15 cm/6 in. Trim the rounds, if necessary, to neaten them.

4 Heat a medium, ungreased griddle or heavy-based frying pan over a moderate heat. Cook the tortillas, one at a time, for about 1½–2 minutes on each side, turning them over when the bottom is pale brown. Stack the tortillas in a clean cloth and serve.

COOK'S TIP

Make flour tortillas if *masa harina* is hard to obtain. To keep them soft and pliable, they must be kept warm, so if you are not eating them right away, wrap in foil and keep them warm in the oven.

Tortilla Flutes with Chicken

These filled tortillas are fried in hot oil until crisp.

Makes about 12

INGREDIENTS
24 freshly prepared unbaked
   flour tortillas
2 tomatoes, peeled
1 small onion, chopped
1 garlic clove, chopped
30-45 ml/2-3 tbsp corn oil
2 freshly cooked chicken breasts,
   skinned and shredded
salt

TO GARNISH
fresh coriander
sliced radishes
salsa

tortillas

tomatoes

onion

garlic

oil

salt

cooked chicken breasts

COOK'S TIP
Cook no more than two flutes at a time - it is important not to overcrowd the pan.

1 Place the unbaked flour tortillas in pairs on a work surface, with one tortilla overlapping its partner by about 5 cm/2 in.

2 Cut the tomatoes in half, squeeze out the seeds and chop the flesh roughly. Put it in a food processor with the onion and garlic; process to a purée. Season with salt to taste.

3 Heat 15 ml/1 tbsp of the oil in a frying pan and cook the tomato purée for a few minutes, stirring to blend the flavours. Remove from the heat and stir in the shredded chicken, mixing well.

4 Spread about 30 ml/2 tbsp of the chicken mixture on each pair of tortillas, roll them up into flutes and secure with a cocktail stick. Heat a little oil in a frying pan and fry the flutes in batches until light brown all over. Drain on kitchen paper and serve, garnished with sprigs of coriander, radishes and salsa.

Sopa Seca de Tortilla con Crema

Although the first two words of this recipe title translate as 'dry soup' it is actually a layered bake of tortilla strips, sauce and cheese.

Serves 6

INGREDIENTS
120 ml/4 fl oz/½ cup corn oil
1 onion, finely chopped
2 garlic cloves, chopped
450 g/1 lb tomatoes, peeled, seeded
    and finely chopped
2.5 ml/½ tsp dried oregano
1.5 ml/¼ tsp sugar
16 small, day-old corn tortillas, cut
    into 1 cm/½ in strips
250 ml/8 fl oz/1 cup double cream
115 g/4 oz/1⅓ cups freshly grated
    Parmesan cheese
salt and freshly ground black pepper

oil   *onion*

garlic

tomatoes   *dried oregano*

sugar

corn tortillas   *double cream*

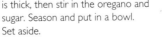

grated Parmesan cheese

1 Heat 30 ml/2 tbsp of oil in a frying pan. Sauté the onion and garlic until soft and stir in the tomatoes.

2 Cook the tomatoes until the sauce is thick, then stir in the oregano and sugar. Season and put in a bowl. Set aside.

COOK'S TIP
Be sure to use corn tortillas for this recipe. If only large ones are available, use eight.

3 Heat the remaining oil in the clean pan and fry the tortilla strips without browning. Drain on kitchen paper.

4 Pour a layer of tomato sauce into a greased flameproof casserole. Add a layer of tortilla strips, a thin layer of cream, another layer of sauce, and a layer of grated cheese. Continue until all the ingredients have been used, ending with a layer of cheese. Cover and heat through gently on top of the stove. (Or heat in a preheated 180°C/350°F/Gas 4 oven for 20 minutes.)

Mixed Tostadas and Quesadillas

Two wonderful ways of using corn tortillas to make tasty snacks.

Makes 14 of each

INGREDIENTS
28 freshly prepared unbaked corn tortillas
oil, for shallow frying

FOR THE TOSTADAS
225 g/8 oz/1 cup mashed red kidney or pinto beans
1 lettuce, shredded
2 cooked chicken breasts, skinned and thinly sliced
225 g/8 oz guacamole
115 g/4 oz/1 cup coarsely grated Cheddar cheese

FOR THE QUESADILLAS
225 g/8 oz/2 cups finely chopped or grated Cheddar cheese
3 *jalapeño* chillies, seeded and cut into strips
shredded lettuce, to garnish

corn tortillas

red kidney beans

cooked chicken breasts

lettuce

guacamole

jalapeño chillies

grated Cheddar cheese

1 To make the tostadas, fry half the tortillas in oil until just crisp. Spread with beans. Put a layer of shredded lettuce over the beans.

2 Add layers of chicken, guacamole and grated cheese. Serve on individual plates and eat using your hands.

3 To make quesadillas, combine the grated cheese and chilli strips in a bowl. Holding an unbaked tortilla on your palm, put a spoonful of filling along the centre, avoiding the edges.

4 Fold the tortilla and seal the edges by pressing or crimping well together. Fry in hot oil, on both sides, until golden brown and crisp. Drain on kitchen paper, transfer to a plate and keep warm while frying the remaining quesadillas. Serve hot, garnished with shredded lettuce.

VARIATION
Quesadillas can also be stuffed with leftover beans and chillies, or chopped chorizo sausage fried with a little chopped onion.

Chilaquiles

This simple casserole of crisply fried tortilla strips layered with a sauce of puréed tomatillos is often served as part of a substantial Mexican breakfast.

Serves 4

INGREDIENTS

corn or peanut oil, for frying
6 freshly prepared, unbaked corn
    tortillas, cut or torn into
    1 cm/^{1}/$_2$ in strips
275 g/10 oz can tomatillos (Mexican
    green tomatoes)
1 onion, finely chopped
2–3 drained canned *jalapeño* chillies,
    rinsed, seeded and chopped
30 ml/2 tbsp chopped fresh coriander
115 g/4 oz/1 cup grated Cheddar
    cheese
175 ml/6 fl oz/^{3}/$_4$ cup chicken stock
salt and freshly ground black pepper

TO GARNISH

thinly sliced mild white onion
stuffed green olives
fresh coriander

oil   corn tortillas   tomatillos

canned jalapeño *chillies*   onion   coriander

grated Cheddar cheese   chicken stock

1 Preheat the oven to 180°C/350°F/Gas 4. Heat 45 ml/3 tbsp oil in a large frying pan. Fry the tortilla strips, a few at a time, on both sides, without browning. Add more oil if needed. Drain on kitchen paper.

2 Tip the tomatillos and the juice from the can into a food processor. Add the onion, chillies and coriander and process to a smooth purée. Season with salt and pepper.

3 Heat 15 ml/1 tbsp oil in the clean frying pan, add the tomatillo purée and cook gently for 2–3 minutes, stirring frequently. Pour a layer of the sauce into a shallow baking dish and top with a layer of tortilla strips and a layer of grated cheese. Continue until all the ingredients have been used, reserving some cheese for sprinkling on top.

4 Pour the chicken stock over the dish and sprinkle with the reserved cheese. Bake, uncovered, for 30 minutes or until heated through. Serve directly from the dish, garnished with thinly sliced onion, olives and coriander.

Red Enchiladas

Chorizo sausages give this layered bake a delicious spicy flavour.

Serves 4

INGREDIENTS

4 *ancho* chillies
450 g/1 lb tomatoes, peeled, seeded
    and chopped
1 onion, finely chopped
1 garlic clove, chopped
15 ml/1 tbsp chopped fresh
    coriander
corn oil, for frying
250 ml/8 fl oz/1 cup soured cream
4 chorizo sausages, skinned
    and chopped
18 freshly prepared unbaked
    corn tortillas
50 g/2 oz/²/₃ cup freshly grated
    Parmesan cheese
salt and freshly ground black pepper

ancho *chillies*

tomatoes

onion   *soured cream*

coriander

garlic

chorizo sausages

corn tortillas   *grated Parmesan
cheese*

1 Roast the *ancho* chillies in a dry frying pan for 1–2 minutes, shaking frequently. When cool, carefully slit the chillies, remove the stems and seeds, and tear the pods into pieces. Put in a bowl, add warm water to just cover, soak for 20 minutes, then tip the chillies, with a little of the soaking water, into a food processor. Add the tomatoes, onion, garlic and coriander; process to a smooth purée.

2 Heat 15 ml/1 tbsp oil in a saucepan. Add the purée and cook over a moderate heat, stirring constantly, for 3–4 minutes. Season to taste with salt and pepper and then stir in the soured cream. Remove the pan from the heat and set it aside.

3 Heat a further 15 ml/1 tbsp oil in a small frying pan; sauté the chorizo for a few minutes, until lightly browned. Moisten with a little of the sauce and set the pan aside.

COOK'S TIP

The method of first dipping the tortillas in sauce, then quickly cooking them in lard or oil gives the best flavour. If you prefer, fry the plain tortillas very quickly, then dip them in the sauce, stuff and roll. There is not a great loss of flavour, and no spatter.

4 Preheat the oven to 180°C/350°F/ Gas 4. Heat 30 ml/2 tbsp oil in a frying pan. Dip a tortilla in the sauce and add to the pan. Cook for a few seconds, shaking the pan gently. Turn over and briefly fry the other side. Slide the tortilla on to a plate, top with some of the sausage mixture, and roll up. Pack the prepared tortillas in a single layer in a baking dish. Pour the sauce over, sprinkle with Parmesan and bake for about 20 minutes.

Chimichangas

For a quick and easy snack, pack tortilla parcels with Picadillo, a wonderful spiced minced mixture. Fry until crisp and golden and serve them straight away while piping hot.

Makes 14

INGREDIENTS
¹/₂ quantity Picadillo
14 freshly prepared unbaked
    flour tortillas
corn oil, for frying
whole radishes with leaves,
    to garnish

Picadillo

flour tortillas

oil

1 Spoon about 60 ml/4 tbsp Picadillo down the centre of each tortilla. Fold in the sides, then the top and bottom, envelope-fashion, or simply roll up and fasten with a cocktail stick.

2 Pour the corn oil into a frying pan to a depth of about 2.5 cm/1 in. Fry the chimichangas, a few at a time, for about 1–2 minutes, or until golden. Drain on kitchen paper and serve, garnished with whole radishes.

COOK'S TIP

Mexican cooks make another delicious snack using the same mixture to stuff *jalapeño* or *poblano* chillies, which are then coated in a light batter before being fried.

Tacos

To make tacos, all you need is a supply of fresh corn tortillas, and as many of the suggested fillings as you can muster. The idea is to use your imagination, and cooks often vie with one another to see who can produce the most interesting combination of flavours.

Makes as many as you like

INGREDIENTS
freshly prepared corn tortillas or
    pre-prepared taco shells

FOR THE FILLINGS
cooked shredded beef, pork
    or chicken with salsa and
    shredded lettuce
Picadillo topped with guacamole
fried chopped chorizo, mixed
    with diced Cheddar cheese
    and chillies
Refried Beans with sliced *jalapeño*
    chillies, guacamole and cubed
    cheese
leftover Mole Poblano de Guajolote
    with guacamole

1 To make traditional soft tacos, spoon the filling on to the tortilla, wrap the tortilla around the filling – and eat. If you prefer hard tacos, secure the rolled up and filled tortilla with a cocktail stick, then briefly shallow fry.

corn tortillas

taco shells

COOK'S TIP

Tacos make perfect party food for your guests to assemble themselves. Provide stacks of warmed tortillas, a selection of fillings and plenty of Mexican beer and you have all you need for a *taquisa*, or taco party.

2 Pre-prepared U-shaped taco shells are more Tex-Mex than truly Mexican, but make a speedy version of this snack. Hold one taco shell at a time and stuff with the fillings of your choice.

Soups

Corn Soup

This is a simple-to-make yet very flavoursome soup.
It is sometimes made with soured cream or cream
cheese. Poblano chillies may be added, but these
are rather difficult to obtain outside Mexico.

Serves 4

INGREDIENTS
30 ml/2 tbsp corn oil
1 onion, finely chopped
1 red pepper, seeded and chopped
450 g/1 lb/2⅔ cups sweetcorn
    kernels, thawed if frozen
750 ml/1¼ pints/3 cups chicken
    stock
250 ml/8 fl oz/1 cup single cream
salt and freshly ground black pepper
½ red pepper, seeded and cut in
    small dice, to garnish

oil

onion

red pepper

sweetcorn kernels

single cream

chicken stock

1 Heat the oil in a frying pan and
sauté the onion and red pepper for
about 5 minutes, until soft. Add the
sweetcorn and sauté for 2 minutes. Tip
the mixture into a food processor or
blender and process until smooth,
adding a little of the stock, if necessary.

2 Put the mixture into a saucepan and
stir in the stock. Season, bring to a
simmer and cook for 5 minutes. Gently
stir in the cream. Serve the soup hot or
chilled, sprinkled with the diced red
pepper. If serving hot, reheat gently, but
do not allow the soup to boil.

Courgette Soup

It takes only minutes to make this delicious soup.
Use the smallest courgettes you can find.

Serves 4

INGREDIENTS
25 g/1 oz/2 tbsp butter
1 onion, finely chopped
450 g/1 lb young courgettes, trimmed
    and chopped
750 ml/1¼ pints/3 cups chicken
    stock
120 ml/4 fl oz/½ cup single cream,
    plus extra to serve
salt and freshly ground black pepper

butter

onion

courgettes

chicken stock

single cream

1 Melt the butter in a saucepan and
sauté the onion until it is soft. Add the
courgettes and cook, stirring, for about
1–2 minutes. Add the chicken stock.
Bring to the boil over a moderate heat
and simmer for about 5 minutes, or
until the courgettes are just tender.

2 Strain the stock into a clean
saucepan, saving the vegetable solids in
the sieve. Purée the solids in a food
processor or blender and add to the
pan. Season to taste with salt and
pepper. Stir the cream into the soup
and heat through very gently without
allowing it to boil. Serve in heated soup
bowls, with a little extra cream swirled
into each portion.

COOK'S TIP
You can use this lovely soup recipe
for other small summer squash.
Mexican courgettes, called
calabacita, are a delicate pale green
and are usually round or pear-shaped.

Vermicelli Soup

The name may not be particularly inspiring, but this soup is delectable.

Serves 4

INGREDIENTS
30 ml/2 tbsp corn oil
50 g/2 oz/¹/₃ cup vermicelli
1 onion, roughly chopped
1 garlic clove, chopped
450 g/1 lb tomatoes, peeled, seeded and roughly chopped
1 litre/1³/₄ pints/4 cups chicken stock
1.5 ml/¹/₄ tsp sugar
15 ml/1 tbsp finely chopped fresh coriander, plus extra to garnish
salt and freshly ground black pepper
25 g/1 oz/¹/₃ cup freshly grated Parmesan cheese, to serve

oil
vermicelli
onion
garlic
tomatoes
chicken stock
coriander
grated Parmesan cheese

COOK'S TIP

Vermicelli burns very easily, so move it about constantly in the frying pan using a wooden spoon and remove it from the heat as soon as it is golden brown.

1 Heat the oil and sauté the vermicelli over a moderate heat until golden brown. Remove with a slotted spoon and drain on kitchen paper.

2 Purée the onion, garlic and tomatoes in a food processor until smooth. Heat the oil remaining in the frying pan and cook the purée, stirring constantly, for 5 minutes or until thick.

3 Transfer the purée to a saucepan. Add the vermicelli, stock, sugar, salt and pepper. Stir in the coriander, bring to the boil, then simmer until the vermicelli is tender. Serve in heated bowls, sprinkled with chopped fresh coriander. Offer the Parmesan separately.

Tomato Soup

Fresh tomato soup is a Mexican favourite, and has a delicately spicy taste.

Serves 4

INGREDIENTS
15 ml/1 tbsp corn oil
1 onion, finely chopped
900 g/2 lb tomatoes, peeled, seeded and chopped
475 ml/16 fl oz/2 cups chicken stock
2 large fresh coriander sprigs
salt and freshly ground black pepper
coarsely ground black pepper, to serve

oil
onion

tomatoes
chicken stock

coriander

COOK'S TIP

Make this fresh-tasting soup in summer when you can buy full-flavoured, outdoor-grown tomatoes.

1 Heat the oil and fry the onion for 5 minutes, until soft and transparent but not brown. Add the tomatoes, stock and coriander. Bring to the boil, then cover the pan and simmer gently for about 15 minutes.

2 Remove and discard the coriander. Press the soup through a sieve and return it to the clean pan. Season to taste and heat through. Serve in heated bowls, sprinkled with coarsely ground black pepper.

Tlalpeño-style Soup

For a hearty version of this simple soup, add some cooked chick-peas or rice.

Serves 6

INGREDIENTS

1.5 litres/2½ pints/6¼ cups chicken stock
2 cooked chicken breast fillets, skinned and cut into large strips
1 drained canned *jalapeño* chilli, rinsed
1 avocado, sliced

chicken stock

cooked chicken breast fillets

canned jalapeño chillies

avocado

1 Heat the stock in a large saucepan and add the chicken and chilli. Simmer for 5 minutes to heat the chicken and release the flavour of the chilli.

2 Remove the chilli from the stock, using a slotted spoon, and then discard it. Pour the soup into heated serving bowls, distributing the chicken evenly among them. Add a few avocado slices to each bowl and serve.

COOK'S TIP

When using canned chillies, rinse them very thoroughly before adding them to the pan to remove the flavour of any pickling liquid.

Avocado Soup

This classic Mexican soup tastes just as good served hot or cold.

Serves 4

INGREDIENTS

2 large ripe avocados
1 litre/1¾ pints/4 cups chicken stock
250 ml/8 fl oz/1 cup single cream
salt and freshly ground white pepper
chopped fresh coriander, to garnish

avocados

chicken stock

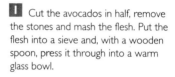

single cream

1 Cut the avocados in half, remove the stones and mash the flesh. Put the flesh into a sieve and, with a wooden spoon, press it through into a warm glass bowl.

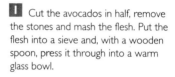

2 Heat the chicken stock with the cream in a saucepan. When the mixture is hot, but not boiling, whisk it into the puréed avocado. Season to taste and serve immediately, sprinkled with plenty of chopped coriander.

COOK'S TIP

The easiest way to mash the avocados is to hold each stoned half in turn in the palm of one hand and mash the flesh in the shell with a fork, before scooping it into the bowl. This avoids the avocado slithering about when it is being mashed.

Frijoles

These highly flavoured cooked beans form the basis of numerous Mexican dishes.

Serves 6-8

INGREDIENTS

350 g/12 oz/1¼–1½ cups dried red
  kidney or pinto beans, picked over
  and rinsed
2 onions, finely chopped
2 garlic cloves, chopped
1 bay leaf
1 or more *serrano* chillies
30 ml/2 tbsp corn oil
2 tomatoes, peeled, seeded and
  chopped
salt
sprigs of fresh bay leaves, to garnish

red kidney beans

onion

garlic

bay leaf

serrano chillies

oil

tomatoes

1 Put the beans into a large saucepan and add cold water to cover by 2.5 cm/ 1 in. Add half the onion, half the garlic, the bay leaf and the chilli(es). Bring to the boil and boil vigorously for about 10 minutes. Lower the heat, cover and continue to cook gently for about 30 minutes. Add boiling water if the mixture starts to become dry.

COOK'S TIP

In Yucatán black haricot beans are used in this recipe, and the Mexican herb *epazote* is added.

2 When the beans begin to wrinkle, add 15 ml/1 tbsp of the corn oil and cook for a further 30 minutes, or until the beans are tender. Add salt to taste and cook for 30 minutes more, but do not add any more water. Remove the bay leaf.

3 Remove the beans from the heat. Heat the remaining oil in a small frying pan and sauté the remaining onion and garlic until the onion is soft. Add the chopped tomatoes and cook for a few minutes more.

4 Spoon 45 ml/3 tbsp of the beans out of the pan and add them to the tomato mixture. Mash to a paste. Stir this into the beans to thicken the liquid. Cook for just long enough to heat through, if necessary. Serve the beans in small bowls and garnish with sprigs of fresh bay leaves.

Peppers Stuffed with Beans

Stuffed peppers are a popular Mexican dish.
A special version – Chiles en Nogada – is served
every year on 28 August to celebrate
Independence Day.

Serves 6

INGREDIENTS
6 large green peppers
30 ml/2 tbsp corn oil, plus extra for
    frying
1 quantity Refried Beans
2 eggs, separated
2.5 ml/¹/₂ tsp salt
plain flour, for coating
120 ml/4 fl oz/¹/₂ cup whipping
    cream
115 g/4 oz/1 cup grated Cheddar
    cheese
fresh coriander sprigs, to garnish

green
peppers

Refried
Beans

flour

eggs

oil

whipping
cream

grated Cheddar cheese

1 Place the peppers on a baking sheet and brush lightly with oil. Grill as close to the heat as possible until blackened all over. Cover with several layers of kitchen paper and set aside.

2 Preheat the oven to 180°C/350°F/ Gas 4. As soon as the peppers are cool enough to handle, peel off the skins. Slit the peppers down one side and remove the seeds and ribs, taking care not to break the pepper shells.

3 Cupping each pepper in turn in your hand, stuff with the refried beans, taking care not to fill the peppers too full. Press gently together.

4 Beat the egg whites in a large bowl until they stand in firm peaks. In another bowl, beat the yolks lightly together with the salt. Fold the yolks gently into the whites. Pour the corn oil into a large frying pan to a depth of about 2.5 cm/ 1 in and heat. Spread out the flour in a shallow bowl or dish.

5 Dip the filled peppers in the flour and then in the egg mixture. Fry in batches until golden brown all over. Arrange the peppers in an ovenproof dish. Pour over the cream and sprinkle with the cheese. Bake for 30 minutes, or until the topping is golden brown and the peppers are heated through. Serve at once, garnished with fresh coriander.

Courgettes with Tomatoes and Chillies

Don't try to rush this – the acid in the tomatoes slows down the cooking of the courgettes.

Serves 4

INGREDIENTS
30 ml/2 tbsp corn oil
450 g/1 lb young courgettes, sliced
1 onion, finely chopped
2 garlic cloves, chopped
450 g/1 lb tomatoes, peeled, seeded and chopped
2 drained canned *jalapeño* chillies, rinsed, seeded and chopped
15 ml/1 tbsp chopped fresh coriander, plus extra to garnish
salt

oil   *courgettes*

onion   *garlic*

tomatoes   *canned* jalapeño *chillies*

coriander

1 Heat the oil in a heavy-based saucepan and add all the remaining ingredients, except the salt and coriander garnish.

2 Simmer, covered, for about 30 minutes, until the courgettes are tender, adding a little tomato juice, stock or water if the dish starts to dry out. Season with salt and serve, garnished with chopped coriander.

Refried Beans

One of the best-known Mexican specialities, this consists of savoury beans mashed with lard or oil. Dense and delicious, the mixture goes well with crisp fried tortillas.

Serves 6-8

INGREDIENTS
75-115 g/3-4 oz/6-8 tbsp lard
1 onion, finely chopped
1 quantity *Frijoles* (cooked beans)

TO SERVE
freshly grated Parmesan cheese or crumbled cottage cheese
crisp fried corn tortillas, cut into quarters

lard   *onion*

Frijoles

grated Parmesan cheese   *tortillas*

1 Heat 25 g/1 oz/2 tbsp of the lard in a large, heavy-based frying pan and sauté the onion until it is soft. Add about 250 ml/8 fl oz/1 cup of the *Frijoles* (cooked beans).

2 Mash the beans, gradually adding more beans and melted lard until all the ingredients are used up and the beans have formed a heavy paste. Tip out on to a warmed platter, piling the mixture up in a roll. Sprinkle with the cheese, spike with tortilla triangles and serve.

COOK'S TIP

Lard is the traditional (and best-tasting) fat for the beans, but many people prefer to use corn oil. Avoid using olive oil, which is too strongly flavoured and distinctive.

Mushrooms with Chillies

These mushrooms bite back! Spiked with chillies, they make a superb salad, starter or cocktail snack.

Serves 6

INGREDIENTS
450 g/1 lb/6 cups button mushrooms
60 ml/4 tbsp olive oil
1 onion, finely chopped
2 garlic cloves, chopped
2 drained canned red chillies, rinsed
    and sliced
salt
chopped fresh coriander, to garnish

mushrooms

olive oil

onion

garlic

canned red chillies

1 Wipe the mushrooms gently and carefully with kitchen paper. Heat the olive oil in a large frying pan and add the mushrooms, finely chopped onion, chopped garlic and sliced chillies. Stir to coat in oil.

2 Fry the mixture over a moderate heat for 6–8 minutes, stirring from time to time, until the onions and mushrooms are tender. Season to taste with salt and serve on small individual plates, sprinkled with a little chopped fresh coriander.

COOK'S TIP
Never wash mushrooms as they quickly absorb water. Wipe them with moistened kitchen paper or a clean, damp cloth.

Prawn Salad

This simple salad has only a flicker of fire, and even that can be eliminated if you wish, by leaving out the *jalapeño* chilli.

Serves 4

INGREDIENTS
60 ml/4 tbsp mayonnaise
60 ml/4 tbsp soured cream
350 g/12 oz cooked, peeled prawns,
    thawed if frozen, chopped
75 g/3 oz/$\frac{1}{2}$ cup cooked green beans,
    chopped
75 g/3 oz/$\frac{1}{2}$ cup cooked carrots,
    chopped
$\frac{1}{2}$ cucumber, chopped
2 hard-boiled eggs, coarsely chopped
1 drained pickled *jalapeño* chilli,
    rinsed, seeded and chopped
salt
Little Gem lettuce, to serve

1 Mix the mayonnaise and soured cream together in a small bowl and set aside.

mayonnaise

soured cream   *cooked prawns*

green beans   *carrots*

jalapeño chillies   *cucumber*

2 Mix the prawns, beans, carrots, cucumber, eggs and chilli in a separate bowl. Season with salt, then fold in the mayonnaise mixture. Pile the mixture on the lined platter and serve with Little Gem lettuce leaves.

hard-boiled eggs

Mexican-style Rice

A hot favourite, this simple dish is colourful and flavoursome. Warn the diners that the elaborate chilli "flowers" used for the garnish are extremely hot and should be approached with caution.

Serves 4

INGREDIENTS
350 g/12 oz/1¾ cups long-grain
    white rice
1 onion, chopped
2 garlic cloves, chopped
450 g/1 lb tomatoes, peeled, seeded
    and coarsely chopped
60 ml/4 tbsp corn oil
900 ml/1½ pints/3¾ cups chicken
    stock
175 g/6 oz/1 cup cooked green peas
salt and freshly ground black pepper
fresh coriander sprigs and red chilli
    "flowers", to garnish

rice

onion

garlic

oil

tomatoes

*chicken
stock*

cooked peas

COOK'S TIP
Other vegetables can be added to the rice if you prefer, such as carrots, courgettes or chopped spinach. Adding some shredded, cooked chicken towards the end of the cooking time would turn it into a main dish.

1 Soak the rice in a bowl of hot water for 15 minutes. Drain in a sieve, rinse well under cold running water, drain again thoroughly and set aside.

2 Combine the onion, garlic and tomatoes in a food processor and process to a purée. Heat the oil in a large frying pan. Add the drained rice and sauté, stirring, until it is golden brown. Using a slotted spoon, transfer the rice to a saucepan.

3 Reheat the oil remaining in the frying pan and cook the tomato purée for 2–3 minutes. Tip it into the saucepan and add the stock. Season to taste. Bring to the boil, reduce the heat to the lowest possible setting, cover the pan and cook for 15–20 minutes, until almost all the liquid has been absorbed.

4 Stir the peas into the rice mixture. Cook, uncovered, until all the liquid has been absorbed and the rice is tender, stirring occasionally. Transfer the rice to a serving dish and garnish with sprigs of coriander and red chilli "flowers".

Broad Beans with Tomatoes and Chillies

In Mexico, lima beans would be used in this tasty dish, but broad beans are just as good – perhaps even better – with the robust sauce.

Serves 4

INGREDIENTS
450 g/1 lb podded broad beans,
    thawed if frozen
30 ml/2 tbsp olive oil
1 onion, finely chopped
2 garlic cloves, chopped
350 g/12 oz tomatoes, peeled, seeded
    and chopped
1 or 2 drained canned *jalapeño*
    chillies, rinsed, seeded and
    chopped
salt
fresh coriander sprigs, to garnish

1 Cook the beans in a saucepan of boiling water for 10–15 minutes, until tender. Drain and keep hot, to one side, in the covered saucepan.

broad beans

olive oil

garlic

onion

canned jalapeño chillies

tomatoes

2 Heat the olive oil in a frying pan and sauté the onion and garlic until the onion is soft but not brown. Add the tomatoes and cook until the mixture is thick and flavoursome.

3 Add the *jalapeño(s)* and cook for 1–2 minutes. Season with salt.

4 Pour the mixture over the reserved beans and check that they are hot. If not, return everything to the frying pan and cook over a low heat for just long enough to heat through. Put into a warm serving dish, garnish with the coriander and serve.

Green Bean and Sweet Red Pepper Salad

Like so many Mexican dishes, this one is very colourful and looks appetizing and pretty on a bed of shredded lettuce.

Serves 4

INGREDIENTS

350 g/12 oz/4 cups cooked green
   beans, quartered
2 red peppers, seeded and chopped
2 spring onions (white and green
   parts), chopped
1 or more drained pickled *serrano*
   chillies, rinsed, seeded and
   chopped
1 iceberg lettuce, coarsely shredded,
   or mixed salad leaves
stuffed olives, to garnish

FOR THE DRESSING

45 ml/3 tbsp red wine vinegar
135 ml/9 tbsp olive oil
salt and freshly ground black pepper

green beans

1 Combine the cooked green beans, chopped peppers, chopped spring onions and chillies in a salad bowl.

2 Make the salad dressing. Pour the red wine vinegar into a jug. Season to taste, then whisk in the olive oil.

3 Pour the salad dressing over the prepared vegetables and toss lightly together to mix and coat thoroughly.

4 Line a large platter with the shredded lettuce or mixed salad leaves and arrange the salad attractively on top. Garnish with the olives and serve.

red pepper

spring onions

red wine vinegar

iceberg lettuce

pickled serrano chillies

olive oil

Avocado and Tomato Salad

Serve this salad as soon as you make it or the avocado slices will discolour.

Serves 4

INGREDIENTS
1 iceberg lettuce, coarsely shredded, or mixed salad leaves
2 large beefsteak tomatoes, about 225 g/8 oz each, peeled, seeded and sliced
2 ripe avocados
30 ml/2 tbsp chopped fresh coriander
salt and freshly ground black pepper

FOR THE DRESSING
90 ml/6 tbsp olive oil
30 ml/2 tbsp fresh lemon juice

iceberg lettuce

beefsteak tomatoes

lemon juice

avocados

coriander

olive oil

1 Spread a bed of shredded lettuce or mixed salad leaves on a large platter and arrange the tomato and avocado slices on top. Sprinkle with the chopped coriander. Season the salad to taste with salt and pepper.

2 Make the dressing. In a jug, whisk the oil and lemon juice together until well combined. Pour a little dressing over the salad to moisten it and serve the rest separately.

COOK'S TIP

To ripen avocados, put them in a brown paper bag and store in a dark place for several days, checking them from time to time. They are ready when they yield to a gentle pressure at the stem end.

Chayote Salad

Chayote goes by several different names – *chocho*, christophine or vegetable pear being the most familiar.

Serves 4

INGREDIENTS
2 chayotes, peeled and halved
1 large beefsteak tomato, about 225 g/8 oz, peeled and cut into 6 wedges
1 small onion, finely chopped
strips of seeded pickled *jalapeño* chillies, plus 2 whole chillies to garnish

FOR THE DRESSING
2.5 ml/½ tsp Dijon mustard
30 ml/2 tbsp mild white vinegar
90 ml/6 tbsp olive oil
salt and freshly ground black pepper

chayotes

beefsteak tomato

onion

pickled jalapeño *chillies*

mustard

white vinegar

olive oil

1 Leaving the seeds in place, cook the chayotes in a large saucepan of boiling salted water for about 20 minutes, or until tender. Drain and leave to cool. Remove the seeds. Cut the flesh into chunks about the same size as the tomato wedges.

2 Make the dressing in the salad bowl. Combine the Dijon mustard and the vinegar with salt and pepper to taste. Gradually whisk in the oil until well combined. Add the chayote, tomato and onion and toss gently. Sprinkle with the chilli strips, garnish with the whole chillies and serve.

Marinated Striped Bass in Spicy Sauce

This is a typical Mayan dish.

Serves 6

INGREDIENTS
1.5 kg/3–3½ lb striped bass, sea bass
   or any non-oily white fish, cut into
   6 steaks
120 ml/4 fl oz/½ cup corn oil
1 large onion, thinly sliced
2 garlic cloves, chopped
350 g/12 oz tomatoes, sliced
2 drained canned *jalapeño* chillies,
   rinsed and sliced
flat leaf parsley, to garnish

FOR THE MARINADE
4 garlic cloves, crushed
5 ml/1 tsp black peppercorns
5 ml/1 tsp dried oregano
2.5 ml/½ tsp ground cumin
5 ml/1 tsp ground *achiote* (annatto)
2.5 ml/½ tsp ground cinnamon
120 ml/4 fl oz/½ cup mild white
   vinegar
salt

oil

sea bass

garlic

onion

tomatoes

canned jalapeño *chillies*

dried oregano

achiote

black peppercorns

ground cumin

ground cinnamon

white vinegar

1 Arrange the fish steaks in a single layer in a shallow dish. Make the marinade. Using a pestle, grind the garlic and black peppercorns in a mortar. Add the dried oregano, cumin, *achiote* (annatto) and cinnamon and mix to a paste with the vinegar. Add salt to taste and spread the marinade on both sides of each of the fish steaks. Cover and leave in a cool place for 1 hour.

2 Select a flameproof dish large enough to hold the fish in a single layer and pour in enough of the oil to coat the bottom. Arrange the fish in the dish with any remaining marinade.

3 Top the fish with the onion, garlic, tomatoes and chillies and pour the rest of the oil over the top.

4 Cover the dish and cook over a low heat on top of the oven for 15–20 minutes, or until the fish is no longer translucent. Serve at once garnished with flat-leaf parsley.

Crab with Green Rice

Green rice is a popular Mexican dish which combines particularly well with crab.

Serves 4

INGREDIENTS
225 g/8 oz/1 generous cup long grain
   rice, soaked in hot water for 15
   minutes
60 ml/4 tbsp olive oil
2 x 275 g/10 oz cans tomatillos
   (Mexican green tomatoes)
1 onion, chopped
2 garlic cloves, chopped
30 ml/2 tbsp chopped fresh
   coriander
about 350 ml/12 fl oz/1½ cups
   chicken stock
450 g/1 lb crab meat, thawed if frozen
salt
chopped fresh coriander, to garnish
lettuce leaves, to serve

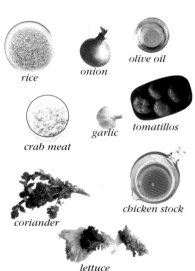

rice · onion · olive oil · crab meat · garlic · tomatillos · coriander · chicken stock · lettuce

1 Drain the rice. Heat the oil in a frying pan and sauté the rice until it is golden and has absorbed the oil. Drain the tomatillos, reserving the juice, put them into a food processor with the onion, garlic and coriander, and process to a purée. Pour into a measuring jug and add the tomatillo juice and enough stock to make the quantity up to 475 ml/16 fl oz/2 cups. Season to taste.

2 Place the rice, tomato mixture and crab meat in a shallow pan. Cover and cook over a very low heat for about 30 minutes, or until the liquid has been absorbed and the rice is tender. Serve on lettuce leaves, garnished with chopped fresh coriander.

COOK'S TIP
Mexican cooks always soak rice in water before cooking it. This seems to pay off, as their rice is always delicious, with every grain separate.

Prawns with Pumpkin Seed Sauce

Ground pumpkin seeds are the secret ingredient in this unusual fish dish.

Serves 4

INGREDIENTS
175 g/6 oz/1 generous cup *pepitas*
   (Mexican pumpkin seeds)
450 g/1 lb raw prawns, thawed if
   frozen, peeled and deveined
1 onion, chopped
1 garlic clove, chopped
30 ml/2 tbsp chopped fresh
   coriander
225 g/8 oz tomatoes, peeled and
   chopped
1 drained canned *jalapeño* chilli,
   rinsed, seeded and chopped
1 red pepper, seeded and chopped
30 ml/2 tbsp corn oil
salt
whole cooked prawns, lemon slices
   and fresh coriander sprigs,
   to garnish
cooked rice, to serve

pumpkin seeds · raw prawns · onion · garlic · coriander · tomatoes · canned jalapeño chillies · oil · red pepper

1 Grind the pumpkin seeds finely, shake through a sieve into a bowl and set aside. Cook the prawns in boiling salted water. As soon as they turn pink, remove with a slotted spoon and set them aside. Reserve the cooking water.

2 Purée the onion, garlic, coriander, tomatoes, chilli, red pepper and ground pumpkin seeds in a food processor. Heat the oil and cook the mixture for 5 minutes. Season. Add prawn water to thin the mixture to a sauce consistency. Add the prawns and heat gently. Garnish and serve with rice.

Seviche

This is an excellent starter. With the addition of sliced avocado, it could make a light summer lunch for four.

Serves 6

INGREDIENTS

450 g/1 lb mackerel fillets, cut into
   1 cm/¹/₂ in pieces
350 ml/12 fl oz/1¹/₂ cups freshly
   squeezed lime or lemon juice
225 g/8 oz tomatoes, chopped
1 small onion, very finely chopped
2 drained canned *jalapeño* chillies or
   4 *serrano* chillies, rinsed and
   chopped
60 ml/4 tbsp olive oil
2.5 ml/¹/₂ tsp dried oregano
30 ml/2 tbsp chopped fresh
   coriander
salt and freshly ground black pepper
lemon wedges and fresh coriander,
   to garnish
stuffed green olives, to serve

mackerel

lime juice

tomatoes

dried oregano

canned jalapeño chillies

coriander

olive oil

onion

COOK'S TIP

Seviche should not be served too cold. Allow it to stand at room temperature for 15 minutes before serving.

1 Put the fish into a glass dish and pour over the lime or lemon juice, making sure that the fish is completely covered. Cover and chill for 6 hours, turning once, by which time the fish will be opaque, "cooked" by the juice.

2 When the fish is opaque, lift it out of the juice and set it aside. Reserve the juice from the marinade.

3 Combine the tomatoes, onion, chillies, oil, oregano and coriander in a bowl. Season, then pour in the reserved citrus juice. Mix well and pour over the fish. Cover and return the seviche to the fridge for about 1 hour. Garnish with lemon wedges and coriander sprigs, and serve with stuffed olives sprinkled with chopped coriander.

Escabeche

This is one of the most famous Mexican dishes. Pickled fish makes a great main course for a summer buffet.

Serves 6

INGREDIENTS

900 g/2 lb white fish fillets
60 ml/4 tbsp freshly squeezed lime
    or lemon juice
300 ml/$\frac{1}{2}$ pint/1$\frac{1}{4}$ cups olive or
    corn oil
2 whole cloves
6 peppercorns
2 garlic cloves
2.5 ml/$\frac{1}{2}$ tsp ground cumin
2.5 ml/$\frac{1}{2}$ tsp dried oregano
2 bay leaves
1 drained canned *jalapeño* chilli,
    rinsed, seeded, and cut into strips
1 onion, thinly sliced
250 ml/8 fl oz/1 cup white wine
    vinegar
salt
fresh herbs, to garnish

*white
fish fillets*

oil

cloves

lime juice

peppercorns

cumin

garlic

oregano

bay leaves

*canned jalapeño
chillies*

*white wine
vinegar*

onion

1 Skin the fish fillets, cut them into six pieces and arrange them in a single layer in a shallow dish. Drizzle the fish with the lime juice. Marinate for 15 minutes, turning the fillets once. Drain the fillets and pat them dry with kitchen paper. Season with salt. Heat 60 ml/4 tbsp of the oil in a frying pan and sauté the fish until lightly golden brown. Transfer to a platter and set aside.

2 Combine the cloves, peppercorns, garlic, cumin, oregano, bay leaves, chilli, onion and vinegar in a pan. Bring to the boil, then simmer for 3–4 minutes.

3 Add the remaining oil and bring to a simmer. Pour over the fish. Cool, cover and chill for 24 hours. To serve, lift out the fillets with a fish slice and arrange on a serving dish. Garnish with fresh herbs.

Prawns in Red Sauce

This dish proves that authentic Mexican food isn't always fiery.

Serves 4

INGREDIENTS
60 ml/4 tbsp corn oil
1 red pepper, seeded and chopped
2 large spring onions (white and green parts), chopped
2 garlic cloves, chopped
450 g/1 lb tomatoes, peeled, seeded and chopped
60 ml/4 tbsp chopped fresh coriander
a little chicken stock
450 g/1 lb cooked prawns, thawed if frozen, peeled and deveined
salt and freshly ground black pepper
fresh coriander, to garnish
cooked rice, to serve (optional)

oil

red pepper

spring onions

garlic

tomatoes

cooked prawns

coriander

1 Heat the oil in a frying pan and sauté the red pepper, spring onions and garlic until the pepper is soft. Add the tomatoes and simmer for about 10 minutes, or until the mixture is thick and flavoursome. Stir in the coriander and season to taste. If the sauce is very thick, thin with chicken stock.

2 Add the prawns and heat through for 2–3 minutes. Be extra careful not to overcook the prawns as they will toughen very quickly. Serve at once, with rice if liked, and garnish with fresh coriander.

Fish in Parsley Sauce

Very different to the more familiar creamy white sauce, this one is robustly flavoured with tomatillos and garlic as well as parsley.

Serves 6

INGREDIENTS
60 ml/4 tbsp olive oil
6 firm-fleshed white fish fillets
275 g/10 oz can tomatillos (Mexican green tomatoes)
1 onion, finely chopped
2 garlic cloves, chopped
50 g/2 oz/1 cup flat leaf parsley, finely chopped
salt and freshly ground black pepper

TO GARNISH
drained canned *serrano* chillies, rinsed, seeded and shredded
sliced black olives

tomatillos

onion

garlic

olive oil

flat leaf parsley

white fish fillets

serrano chillies

black olives

COOK'S TIP
Flat leaf or continental parsley has much more flavour than curly parsley. Keep the curly variety for use as a decoration and use the flat leaf parsley in cooking.

1 Heat the oil and sauté the fish fillets until they are golden brown on both sides. Transfer the fillets to a warmed serving dish, cover and keep hot. Drain the tomatillos, reserving the liquid. Mash them in a bowl with the onion, garlic and parsley.

2 Heat the oil remaining in the pan and cook the tomatillo mixture gently, stirring occasionally, until the sauce is well blended. If it is too thick, add a little of the reserved tomatillo juice. Season the sauce, pour it over the fish, garnish with the *serrano* chillies and black olives and serve.

Red Snapper, Veracruz-style

This is Mexico's best-known fish dish. In Veracruz red snapper is always used, but fillets of any firm-fleshed white fish can be substituted successfully.

Serves 4

INGREDIENTS

4 large red snapper fillets
30 ml/2 tbsp freshly squeezed lime
   juice
120 ml/4 fl oz/½ cup olive oil
1 onion, finely chopped
2 garlic cloves, chopped
675 g/1½ lb tomatoes, peeled and
   chopped
1 bay leaf, plus a few sprigs to garnish
1.5 ml/¼ tsp dried oregano
30 ml/2 tbsp large capers, plus extra
   to serve (optional)
16 stoned green olives, halved
2 drained canned *jalapeño* chillies,
   rinsed, seeded and cut into strips
butter, for frying
3 slices firm white bread, cut into
   triangles
salt and freshly ground black pepper

red snapper
olive oil
lime juice
tomatoes
onion
garlic
dried oregano
capers
bay leaves
green olives
canned jalapeño *chillies*
butter
bread slices

1 Arrange the fish fillets in a single layer in a shallow dish. Season with salt and pepper, drizzle with the lime juice and set aside.

2 Heat the oil in a large frying pan and sauté the onion and garlic until soft. Add the tomatoes and cook for about 10 minutes, stirring occasionally, until the mixture is thick and flavoursome.

3 Stir in the bay leaf, oregano, capers, olives and chillies. Add the fish and cook over a very low heat for 10 minutes, or until tender.

4 While the fish is cooking, heat the butter in a small frying pan and sauté the bread triangles until they are golden brown on both sides. Transfer the fish to a heated platter, pour over the sauce and surround with the fried bread triangles. Garnish with bay leaves and serve with extra capers, if you like.

Red Snapper and Coriander

Although red snapper is used in this dish, you can use any fillets of firm white fish instead.

Serves 4

INGREDIENTS
900g/2lb red snapper fillets or other
    white fish fillets
90ml/6 tbsp lime or lemon juice
60ml/4 tbsp olive oil
1 onion, finely chopped
50g/2oz/1 cup fresh coriander,
    finely chopped
2 drained canned *jalapeño* chillies,
    rinsed, seeded and sliced
salt and freshly ground black pepper
tomato rice, to serve

red snapper

lime juice

olive oil

onion   *coriander*

canned jalapeño *chillies*

1 Place the fish in a shallow dish. Season with salt and pepper and drizzle the lime or lemon juice over. Cover and set aside for 15 minutes. Preheat the oven to 180°C/350°F/ Gas 4. Heat all but 15ml/1 tbsp of the oil in a frying pan and sauté the onion until it is soft.

2 Use the reserved oil to thinly coat the bottom of an ovenproof dish which is just large enough to hold the fish fillets in a single layer. Arrange the fish in the dish and pour over any of the remaining marinating liquid. Top with the sautéed onion and the oil from the pan.

3 Sprinkle over the coriander and chillies. Bake for 20-25 minutes, or until the fish is no longer translucent. Serve with tomato rice.

TOMATO RICE

To make Tomato Rice simply soak 225 g/8 oz/1 generous cup long grain rice in hot water for 15 minutes, then cook in 475 ml/16 fl oz/2 cups water or stock for 30 minutes. Add some chopped, skinned fresh tomato, salt and pepper. Serve immediately.

Pheasant in Green Pipian Sauce

Pheasant gets an exciting and original treatment in this recipe from Yucatán.

Serves 4

INGREDIENTS
2 oven-ready pheasants
30 ml/2 tbsp corn oil
175 g/6 oz/1 generous cup *pepitas* (Mexican pumpkin seeds)
15 ml/1 tbsp *achiote* (annatto) seeds
1 onion, finely chopped
2 garlic cloves, chopped
275 g/10 oz can tomatillos (Mexican green tomatoes)
475 ml/16 fl oz/2 cups chicken stock
salt and freshly ground black pepper
fresh coriander, to garnish

pheasants

pumpkin seeds

chicken stock

garlic

oil

onion

tomatillos

coriander

1 Preheat the oven to 180°C/350°F/Gas 4. Using a large, sharp knife or poultry shears, cut the pheasants in half lengthways and season well with salt and pepper. Heat the oil in a large frying pan and sauté the pieces until lightly brown on all sides. Lift out, drain and arrange, skin-side up, in a roasting tin large enough to hold them comfortably in one layer. Set aside.

2 Grind the pumpkin seeds finely in a nut grinder or a food processor. Shake through a sieve into a bowl. Grind the achiote seeds, add them to the bowl and set to one side. Put the onion and garlic in a food processor. Add the tomatillos with their juice and process to a smooth purée. Scrape into a saucepan.

3 Add the pumpkin seed mixture, stir in the stock and simmer over a very low heat for 10 minutes. Do not let the mixture boil as it will separate. Remove from the heat and allow to cool.

4 Pour the sauce over the pheasant halves. Bake for 40 minutes, or until tender, basting from time to time with the sauce. Garnish with coriander and serve immediately.

Chicken in Green Almond Sauce

The combination of ground almonds and tomatillos works extremely well.

Serves 6

INGREDIENTS

1.5 kg/3–3½ lb chicken, cut into
    serving pieces
475 ml/16 fl oz/2 cups chicken stock
1 onion, chopped
1 garlic clove, chopped
115 g/4 oz/2 cups fresh coriander,
    coarsely chopped
1 green pepper, seeded and chopped
1 *jalapeño* chilli, seeded and
    chopped
275 g/10 oz can tomatillos (Mexican
    green tomatoes)
115 g/4 oz/1 cup ground almonds
30 ml/2 tbsp corn oil
salt
fresh coriander, to garnish

chicken

chicken stock

onion

garlic

coriander

green pepper

ground almonds

jalapeño chillies

tomatillos

oil

COOK'S TIP
If the colour of the sauce seems a little pale, add 2–3 outer leaves of dark green cos lettuce. Cut out the central ribs, chop the leaves and add to the food processor with the other ingredients. This will lift the colour without altering the flavour.

1 Put the chicken pieces into a flameproof casserole or shallow pan. Pour in the stock, bring to a simmer, cover and cook for about 45 minutes, until tender. Drain the stock into a measuring jug and set aside.

4 Make the reserved stock up to 475 ml/16 fl oz/2 cups with water, if necessary. Stir it into the casserole or pan. Mix gently and simmer just long enough to blend the flavours and heat the chicken pieces through. Add salt to taste. Serve at once, garnished with coriander and accompanied by rice.

2 Put the onion, garlic, coriander, green pepper, chilli, tomatillos with their juice and the almonds into a food processor. Purée fairly coarsely.

3 Heat the oil in a frying pan, add the almond mixture and cook over a low heat, stirring with a wooden spoon, for 3–4 minutes. Scrape into the casserole or pan with the chicken.

Mole Poblano de Guajolote

This is the great festive dish of Mexico. It is served at any special occasion, be it a birthday, wedding or family get-together.

Serves 6-8

INGREDIENTS
1 onion
1 garlic clove
2.75-3.6 kg/6-8 lb turkey, cut into
    serving pieces
90 ml/6 tbsp lard
fresh coriander and 30 ml/2 tbsp
    toasted sesame seeds, to garnish

FOR THE SAUCE
6 *ancho* chillies
4 *pasilla* chillies
4 *mulato* chillies
450 g/1 lb tomatoes, peeled and
    chopped
2 onions, chopped
2 garlic cloves, chopped
1 stale tortilla, torn into pieces
50 g/2 oz/$\frac{1}{3}$ cup seedless raisins
115 g/4 oz/1 cup ground almonds
45 ml/3 tbsp sesame seeds, ground
2.5 ml/$\frac{1}{2}$ tsp coriander seeds, ground
5 ml/1 tsp ground cinnamon
2.5 ml/$\frac{1}{2}$ tsp ground star anise
1.5 ml/$\frac{1}{4}$ tsp ground black
    peppercorns
60 ml/4 tbsp corn oil
40 g/1$\frac{1}{2}$ oz unsweetened (bitter)
    chocolate, broken into squares
15 ml/1 tbsp granulated sugar
salt and freshly ground pepper

I Chop the onion and garlic and put in a large saucepan. Add the turkey pieces, then pour in cold water to cover. Season with salt, bring to a gentle simmer, cover and cook for about 1 hour, or until the turkey is tender.

pasilla *chillies*

mulato *chillies*

tomatoes

tortilla

raisins

ground almonds

coriander seeds

onion

ground black peppercorns

sesame seeds

ground cinnamon

ground star anise

turkey

garlic   ancho *chillies*   *lard*   *chocolate*   *sugar*   *oil*

2 Meanwhile, put the *ancho*, *pasilla* and *mulato* chillies in a dry frying pan over gentle heat and roast them for a few minutes, shaking the pan frequently. Remove the stems and seeds. Tear the pods into pieces and put these into a small bowl with warm water to cover. Soak for 30 minutes, until soft.

4 Make the sauce. Put the tomatoes in a food processor and add the chillies, with the water in which they have been soaked. Tip in the onions, garlic, tortilla, raisins, ground almonds and spices. Process to a purée. Do this in batches if necessary.

3 Lift out the turkey pieces and pat them dry with kitchen paper. Reserve the stock in a measuring jug. Heat the lard in a large frying pan and sauté the turkey pieces until lightly browned all over. Transfer to a plate and set aside.

COOK'S TIP
Roasting the dried chillies lightly brings out the flavour and is worth the extra effort.

5 Add the oil to the fat remaining in the frying pan used for sautéing the turkey. Heat, then add the chilli and spice paste. Cook, stirring, for 5 minutes.

6 Transfer the mixture to a large saucepan. Stir in 475 ml/16 fl oz/2 cups of the turkey stock, add the chocolate and season well. Cook over a low heat until the chocolate has melted. Stir in the sugar. Add the turkey and more stock if needed. Cover the pan and simmer very gently for 30 minutes. Serve, garnished with fresh coriander and sprinkled with the sesame seeds.

Lamb Stew with Mixed Chillies

This stew is known as Estofado de Carnero in Mexico and has an interesting mix of chillies – the mild, full-flavoured *ancho*, and the piquant *jalapeño* which gives extra "bite".

Serves 4

INGREDIENTS

3 *ancho* chillies
30 ml/2 tbsp olive oil
1 *jalapeño* chilli, seeded and chopped
1 onion, finely chopped
2 garlic cloves, chopped
450 g/1 lb tomatoes, peeled and chopped
50 g/2 oz/¹/₃ cup seedless raisins
2.5 ml/¹/₂ tsp ground cinnamon
900 g/2 lb boneless lamb, cut into 5 cm/2 in cubes
250 ml/8 fl oz/1 cup lamb stock or water
salt and freshly ground black pepper
a few fresh coriander sprigs, to garnish
coriander rice, to serve

ancho *chillies*

garlic

onion

olive oil

jalapeño *chillies*

tomatoes

raisins

ground cinnamon

lamb   *lamb stock*   *coriander*

1 Roast the *ancho* chillies lightly in a dry frying pan. Remove the stems and seeds and tear the pods into pieces, then put them into a bowl with warm water to cover. Leave to soak for 30 minutes, until soft.

2 Heat the olive oil in a frying pan and sauté the *jalapeño* chilli with the onion and garlic until the onion is tender. Add the chopped tomatoes, raisins and ground cinnamon. Cook until the mixture is thick and flavoursome, season and transfer to a flameproof casserole.

3 Tip the *ancho* chillies and their soaking water into a food processor and process to a smooth purée. Add the chilli pureé to the tomato mixture in the casserole.

4 Add the lamb cubes to the casserole, stir to mix and pour in enough of the lamb stock or water to just cover the meat. Bring to a simmer, then cover the casserole and cook over a low heat for about 2 hours, or until the lamb is tender. Garnish with fresh coriander sprigs and serve with boiled rice, tossed with chopped fresh coriander.

Mexican Meatballs

Mexican cooks use twice-ground beef and pork for these meatballs, which they call *Albondigas*.

Cook's Tip
The meatballs can be simply poached in beef stock if you prefer. Alternatively, you can use fresh tomato sauce or salsa, thinned down with beef stock.

Serves 4

INGREDIENTS
225 g/8 oz lean minced beef
225 g/8 oz minced pork
50 g/2 oz/1 cup fresh white
  breadcrumbs
1 onion, finely chopped
2.5 ml/½ tsp dried oregano
1 egg, lightly beaten
milk (optional)
corn oil, for frying
salt and freshly ground black pepper
fresh oregano leaves, to garnish

FOR THE SAUCE
beef stock
1 fresh red *jalapeño* or *serrano* chilli,
  seeded and chopped
1 onion, finely chopped
2 garlic cloves, crushed
225 g/8 oz tomatoes, peeled, seeded
  and finely chopped

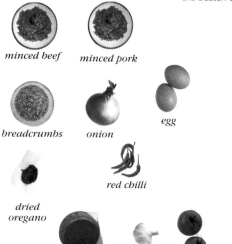

minced beef   *minced pork*

breadcrumbs   *onion*   *egg*

dried oregano   *red chilli*

beef stock   *garlic*   *tomatoes*

1 Put the minced beef and pork through a mincer or process in a food processor so that the mixture is finely minced. Tip it into a bowl and add the breadcrumbs, onion and oregano. Season with salt and pepper and stir in the beaten egg.

2 Knead thoroughly with clean hands to make a smooth mixture, adding a little milk if necessary. Shape the mixture into 4 cm/1½ in balls.

3 Heat 1 cm/½ in oil in a frying pan and fry the balls for 5 minutes, turning occasionally, until browned. Remove from the pan using a slotted spoon and drain on kitchen paper.

4 Put the meatballs into a shallow pan or flameproof casserole and pour over beef stock to cover. Add the remaining sauce ingredients and bring to the boil. Simmer for about 30 minutes. Using a slotted spoon, transfer the meatballs to a serving dish. Press the sauce through a sieve, then spoon it over the meatballs. Serve at once, garnished with oregano.

Beef with Cactus Pieces

Nopalitos – chunks of the edible prickly pear cactus – are used as a vegetable in Mexico, and are the basis of several salads, soups and bakes.

Serves 6

INGREDIENTS

900 g/2 lb braising beef, cut into
    5 cm/2 in cubes`
30 ml/2 tbsp corn oil
1 onion, finely chopped
2 garlic cloves, chopped
1 or 2 *jalapeño* chillies, seeded and
    chopped
115 g/4 oz can *nopalitos* (cactus
    pieces), rinsed and drained
2 x 275 g/10 oz cans tomatillos
    (Mexican green tomatoes)
50 g/2 oz/½ cup chopped fresh
    coriander, plus extra to garnish
beef stock (optional)
salt and freshly ground black pepper

braising beef

oil

garlic   *onion*

jalapeño
chillies   *coriander*

tomatillos

1   Pat the beef cubes dry with kitchen paper. Heat the oil in a frying pan and sauté the beef cubes, a few at a time, until browned all over. Using a slotted spoon, transfer the beef cubes to a flameproof casserole or pan.

2   Add the onion and garlic to the oil remaining in the frying pan and sauté until tender. Add more oil if necessary. Transfer the onions and garlic to the casserole or pan and add the chilli(es).

3   Add the *nopalitos* and tomatillos, with their juice, to the casserole. Stir in the chopped coriander until well mixed. If more liquid is needed to cover the beef, stir in some beef stock. Season with salt and pepper.

4   Bring to a slow simmer, cover and cook over a low heat for about 2½ hours, or until the beef is very tender. Transfer to a warmed dish and serve sprinkled with chopped coriander.

Pork with Pineapple

Tender chunks of pork are combined with warming chillies and cooling pineapple in this simple casserole.

Serves 6

INGREDIENTS
30 ml/2 tbsp corn oil
900 g/2 lb boneless pork shoulder or
    loin, cut into 5 cm/2 in cubes
1 onion, finely chopped
1 large red pepper, seeded and
    finely chopped
1 or more *jalapeño* chillies, seeded
    and finely chopped
450 g/1 lb fresh pineapple chunks
8 fresh mint leaves, chopped
250 ml/8 fl oz/1 cup chicken stock
salt and freshly ground black pepper
fresh mint sprig, to garnish
cooked rice, to serve

oil

pork

red pepper

onion

jalapeño chillies

pineapple

chicken stock

mint leaves

1 Heat the oil in a large frying pan and sauté the pork in batches until the cubes are lightly coloured. Transfer the pork to a flameproof casserole, leaving the oil behind in the pan.

2 Add the finely chopped onion, finely chopped red pepper and the chilli(es) to the oil remaining in the pan. Sauté until the onion is tender, then add to the casserole with the pineapple. Stir to mix.

3 Add the mint and stock, with salt and pepper to taste. Cover and simmer gently for about 2 hours, or until the pork is tender. Garnish with fresh mint and serve with rice.

COOK'S TIP

If fresh pineapple is not available, use pineapple canned in its own juice.

Veal in Nut Sauce

This simple treatment of veal works just as well for pork or even turkey.

Serves 6

INGREDIENTS
1.5 kg/3-3½ lb boneless veal, cut into
    5 cm/2 in cubes
2 onions, finely chopped
1 garlic clove, crushed
2.5 ml/½ tsp dried thyme
2.5 ml/½ tsp dried oregano
350 ml/12 fl oz/1½ cups chicken
    stock
115 g/4 oz/1 cup very finely ground
    almonds, pecan nuts or peanuts
175 g/6 fl oz/¾ cup soured cream
fresh oregano, to garnish
cooked rice, to serve (optional)

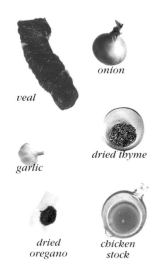

veal

onion

garlic

dried thyme

dried oregano

chicken stock

soured cream

ground almonds

1 Put the veal, onions, garlic, thyme, oregano and chicken stock into a large, flameproof casserole. Bring to a gentle boil. Cover tightly and simmer over a low heat for about 2 hours, or until the veal is cooked and tender.

2 Put the ground nuts in a food processor. Pour in 120 ml/4 fl oz/½ cup of the veal liquid and process for a few seconds, until smooth. Press through a sieve into the casserole. Stir in the soured cream and heat through gently, without boiling. Serve at once, garnished with fresh oregano and accompanied by cooked rice, if liked.

Picadillo

Serve as a main dish with rice, or use to stuff peppers or fill tacos.

Serves 6

INGREDIENTS
30 ml/2 tbsp olive or corn oil
900 g/2 lb minced beef
1 onion, finely chopped
2 garlic cloves, chopped
2 eating apples
450 g/1 lb tomatoes, peeled, seeded
    and chopped
2 or 3 drained pickled *jalapeño*
    chillies, rinsed, seeded and
    chopped
65 g/2½ oz/scant ½ cup raisins
1.5 ml/¼ tsp ground cinnamon
1.5 ml/¼ tsp ground cumin
salt and freshly ground black pepper
tortilla chips, to serve

TO GARNISH
15 g/½ oz/1 tbsp butter
25 g/1 oz/⅓ cup slivered almonds

oil

onion

minced beef

apples

garlic

tomatoes

jalapeño chillies

raisins

ground cinnamon

ground cumin

1 Heat the oil in large frying pan and add the beef, onion and garlic. Fry, stirring from time to time, until the beef is brown and the onion is tender.

2 Peel, core and chop the apples. Add them to the frying pan with the tomatoes, chillies, raisins, cinnamon, cumin and seasoning. Cook, uncovered, for about 20–25 minutes, stirring occasionally. Just before serving, melt the butter and sauté the almonds until golden brown. Serve the Picadillo topped with the almonds and accompanied by the tortilla chips.

DESSERTS

Kings' Day Bread

On 6 January, the day the Three Kings traditionally brought gifts to the infant Jesus, Mexicans also exchange gifts, and serve this iced cake-bread.

Serves 8

INGREDIENTS

10 ml/2 tsp active dry yeast
120 ml/4 fl oz/$\frac{1}{2}$ cup lukewarm water
275 g/10 oz/2$\frac{1}{2}$ cups plain flour
2.5 ml/$\frac{1}{2}$ tsp salt
50 g/2 oz/$\frac{1}{4}$ cup granulated sugar
2 eggs, well beaten
4 egg yolks, lightly beaten
115 g/4 oz/$\frac{1}{2}$ cup unsalted butter, softened
350 g/12 oz/2 cups mixed chopped crystallized fruit and peel
melted butter, for glazing
175 g/6 oz/1$\frac{1}{2}$ cups icing sugar, sifted
30 ml/2 tbsp single cream
glacé cherries, halved, to decorate

yeast

plain flour

sugar

salt

eggs

crystallized fruit and peel

butter

glacé cherries

icing sugar

single cream

1 Sprinkle the yeast over the water, stir and leave for about 5 minutes, or until the mixture is frothy.

2 Put 150 g/5 oz/1$\frac{1}{4}$ cups of the flour in a bowl. Add the salt, sugar, eggs, egg yolks, butter and yeast. Mix well. Put 225 g/8 oz/1$\frac{1}{3}$ cups of the crystallized fruit and peel and 50 g/2 oz/$\frac{1}{2}$ cup of the flour into a bowl and toss to coat. Add to the yeast mixture with the rest of the flour. Beat well to make a soft but not sticky dough.

3 Turn the dough on to a lightly floured board. Knead until smooth.

4 Shape the dough into a ring, place on a greased baking sheet, cover lightly with a cloth and leave in a warm, draught-free place for up to 2 hours, or until it has doubled in size.

5 Preheat the oven to 180°C/350°F/ Gas 4. Brush the ring with melted butter and bake for 30 minutes. Cool. Make the icing by mixing the icing sugar with the cream. Drizzle it over the cold ring. Decorate with the remaining crystallized fruit and peel and the glacé cherries.

Churros

Fabulous fritters that melt in the mouth, Churros are irresistible.

Makes about 24

INGREDIENTS
250 ml/8 fl oz/1 cup water
15 ml/1 tbsp granulated sugar, plus
    extra for dusting
2.5 ml/½ tsp salt
175 g/6 oz/1½ cups plain flour
1 large egg, beaten
oil, for deep frying

sugar

salt

plain flour

egg

oil

1 Bring the water, sugar and salt to the boil in a saucepan. Remove from the heat, beat in the flour until smooth, then beat in the egg, until the mixture is satiny. Spoon the batter into a pastry bag fitted with a fluted nozzle.

2 Heat the oil in a deep-frying pan. Pipe 7.5 cm/3 in strips of batter and then add them to the oil, a few at a time. Fry for 3–4 minutes, or until golden brown. Drain the churros on kitchen paper, roll them in sugar and serve.

COOK'S TIP
You can use a funnel to shape the churros. Close the end with a finger, add the batter, then release into the oil in small columns.

Sopaipillas

Sopaipillas look like squares of sunshine and taste heavenly, especially when drizzled with a little runny honey or syrup.

Makes about 30

INGREDIENTS
225 g/8 oz/2 cups plain flour
15 ml/1 tbsp baking powder
5 ml/1 tsp salt
30 ml/2 tbsp lard
175 ml/6 fl oz/¾ cup water
corn oil, for frying
honey or syrup, to serve

plain flour   *baking powder*

 salt   *lard*

oil    *honey*

1 Put the flour, baking powder and salt into a large bowl. Rub in the lard, then add enough water to form a soft but not sticky dough.

3 Fry the squares, a few at a time, in hot oil. As they brown and puff up, turn over to cook the other side. Drain on kitchen paper and serve warm, with honey or syrup.

2 Knead the dough lightly. Roll it out thinly to a rectangle measuring about 45 × 35 cm/18 × 14 in. Cut into about 30 × 7.5 cm/3 in squares.

Caramel Custard

This is a classic dessert in Mexico, where it is known simply as *flan*.

Serves 6

INGREDIENTS
275 g/10 oz/1¼ cups granulated
    sugar
6 eggs, lightly beaten
1 litre/1¾ pints/4 cups hot milk
5 ml/1 tsp vanilla essence
pinch of salt

**granulated
sugar**

milk

eggs

**vanilla
essence**

salt

1 Preheat the oven to 180°C/350°F/
Gas 4. Melt 115 g/4 oz/½ cup of the
sugar in a small heavy-based saucepan,
stirring constantly. Continue to heat the
sugar syrup, without stirring, until it turns
a deep golden colour, then carefully
coat the bottom and sides of six
ramekins. As soon as the caramel sets,
turn the ramekins upside-down on a
baking sheet.

2 Gradually beat the remaining sugar
into the eggs. Add the cooled milk,
vanilla essence and salt. Mix well. Strain
the egg mixture into the ramekins and
put them into a roasting tin. Add
enough hot water to come halfway up
the sides of the ramekins.

3 Bake for about 40 minutes, or until
a knife inserted in the centre of the
custard comes out clean. Cool, then chill
for several hours in the fridge. To serve,
slide a dampened knife between the
custard and the side of each ramekin.
Turn out on dessert plates.

COOK'S TIP

Flan can also be cooked in one large
bowl and you may be able to find one
of the specially-made tins which have
a clever device to help remove the
cooked *flan* from the tin. Otherwise
it is probably safer to cook them in
individual ramekins.

Almond Biscuits

Traditionally served at weddings, these biscuits literally melt in the mouth.

Makes about 24

INGREDIENTS

115 g/4 oz/1 cup plain flour, sifted
175 g/6 oz/1½ cups icing sugar, sifted, plus extra for dusting
1.5 ml/¼ tsp salt
50 g/2 oz/½ cup almonds, finely chopped
2.5 ml/½ tsp vanilla essence
115 g/4 oz/½ cup unsalted butter, softened

plain flour

icing sugar

salt

ground almonds

vanilla essence

butter

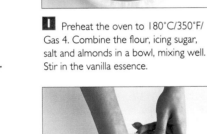

1 Preheat the oven to 180°C/350°F/ Gas 4. Combine the flour, icing sugar, salt and almonds in a bowl, mixing well. Stir in the vanilla essence.

2 Using your fingertips, work the butter into the mixture to make a dough. Form it into a ball.

3 Roll out the dough on a lightly floured surface to a thickness of 3 mm/⅛ in. Using a round cutter, stamp out into about 24 biscuits, re-rolling the trimmings as necessary.

4 Transfer the biscuits to baking sheets and bake for 30 minutes, or until they are delicately browned. Cool on wire racks and dust thickly with icing sugar before serving.

COOK'S TIP
The biscuits can be varied by using other nuts such as walnuts, peanuts or pecan nuts, or by adding spices of your choice.

Buñuelos

If you like doughnuts, you'll love these delicious golden fritters.

Serves 6

INGREDIENTS
225 g/8 oz/2 cups plain flour
2.5 ml/½ tsp salt
5 ml/1 tsp baking powder
15 ml/1 tbsp granulated sugar
1 large egg, beaten
120 ml/4 fl oz/½ cup milk
25 g/1 oz/2 tbsp unsalted butter,
  melted
oil, for deep frying
caster sugar, for dusting

FOR THE SYRUP
225 g/8 oz/1 cup soft light brown
  sugar
750 ml/1¼ pints/3 cups water
2.5 cm/1 in cinnamon stick
1 clove

plain flour

baking powder

salt

granulated sugar

egg

milk

oil

butter

cinnamon

brown sugar

clove

1 Make the syrup. Mix the sugar and water in a saucepan. Heat, stirring, until the sugar has dissolved, then add the spices and simmer until the mixture has reduced to a light syrup. Remove and discard the spices. Keep the syrup warm while you make the *buñuelos*.

2 Sift the flour, salt and baking powder into a bowl. Stir in the granulated sugar. In a mixing bowl, whisk the egg and the milk well together. Gradually stir in the dry mixture, then beat in the melted butter to make a soft dough.

3 Turn the dough on to a lightly floured board and knead until it is smooth and elastic. Divide the dough into 18 even-size pieces. Shape into balls. With your hands, flatten the balls to disc shapes about 2 cm/¾ in thick.

4 Use the floured handle of a wooden spoon to poke a hole through the centre of each *buñuelo*. Heat the oil for deep frying to a temperature of 190°C/375°F, or until a cube of day-old bread added to the oil browns in 30–60 seconds.

5 Fry the fritters in batches, taking care not to overcrowd the pan, until they are puffy and golden brown on both sides. Lift out with a slotted spoon and drain on kitchen paper. Dust the *buñuelos* with caster sugar and serve with the syrup.

COOK'S TIP
Make the syrup ahead of time if you prefer, and chill it until ready to use, when it can be warmed through quickly.

Pumpkin in Brown Sugar

Slow-cooked pumpkin is sweet and tender. Serve this unusual dessert with plain yogurt or whipped cream.

Serves 4

INGREDIENTS
900 g/2 lb pumpkin, cut
    into wedges
350 g/12 oz/1½ cups soft dark
    brown sugar
about 120 ml/4 fl oz/½ cup water
plain yogurt or whipped cream,
    to serve

pumpkin

brown sugar

I Scrape the seeds out of the pumpkin wedges. Pack the wedges firmly together in a heavy-based, flameproof casserole.

2 Divide the sugar among the pumpkin pieces, packing it into the hollows which contained the seeds.

3 Pour the water carefully into the the casserole to cover the bottom and prevent the pumpkin from burning. Take care not to dislodge the sugar when pouring in the water.

4 Cover and cook over a low heat, checking the water level frequently, until the pumpkin is tender and the sugar has dissolved in the liquid to form a sauce. Serve at once with plain yogurt, sweetened with a little brown sugar, if you like, or with whipped cream.

COOK'S TIP

The best pumpkin for this recipe is the classic orange-fleshed variety used to make Hallowe'en lanterns. Choose one which will fit neatly into your casserole when cut into wedges.

Coconut Custard

Fresh coconut gives this custard a fabulously rich flavour and texture.

Serves 6

INGREDIENTS

225 g/8 oz/1 cup granulated sugar
250 ml/8 fl oz/1 cup water
7.5 cm/3 in cinnamon stick
115 g/4 oz/1 cup grated fresh
    coconut
750 ml/1¼ pints/3 cups milk
4 eggs
175 ml/6 fl oz/³/₄ cup whipping
    cream
45 ml/3 tbsp toasted chopped
    almonds (optional)

sugar

cinnamon stick

coconut

milk

eggs

whipping cream

COOK'S TIP

The easiest way to prepare a fresh coconut is to bake it in a preheated 180°C/350°F/ Gas 4 oven for 15 minutes, then pierce two of the eyes with an ice-pick or sharp skewer and drain out the milk. Open the coconut by hitting it carefully with a hammer; it will break into several pieces, making it easy to remove the shell. Peel off the brown skin, chop the flesh into small pieces and grate in a food processor.

1 Combine the sugar, water and cinnamon stick in a large saucepan. Bring to the boil, then lower the heat and simmer, uncovered, for 5 minutes. Remove the cinnamon stick.

2 Add the grated coconut to the pan, and cook over a low heat for 5 minutes more. Stir in the milk and cook, stirring from time to time, until the mixture has thickened to the consistency of thin custard. Remove from the heat and set aside.

3 In a bowl, beat the eggs until fluffy. Stir in a ladleful of the coconut mixture. Continue to add the coconut mixture in this way, then return the contents of the bowl to the clean pan and stir over a low heat until the mixture becomes a thick custard.

4 Pour the custard into a serving dish, allow to cool, then chill until ready to serve. Just before serving, whip the cream until thick and spread it over the custard. Decorate with the toasted chopped almonds, if using.

Rompope

This drink could best be described as cooked eggnog. It keeps well if chilled, though it seldom gets the chance.

Makes about
1.75 litres/3 pints/
7½ cups

INGREDIENTS
1 litre/1³/₄ pints/4 cups milk
225 g/8 oz/1 cup granulated sugar
5 cm/2 in cinnamon stick
50 g/2 oz/¹/₂ cup ground almonds
12 large egg yolks
475 ml/16 fl oz/2 cups rum

milk

sugar

cinnamon
stick

ground
almonds

egg yolks

rum

1 Combine the milk, sugar and cinnamon in a large saucepan. Simmer over a very low heat, stirring, until the sugar has dissolved. Cool to room temperature. Remove the cinnamon stick and stir in the ground almonds.

2 Beat the egg yolks until they are very thick and pale. Add to the almond mixture a little at a time, beating well. Return the pan to the heat and cook gently until the mixture coats a spoon. Cool, then stir in the rum. Pour into a clean dry bottle and cork tightly. Keep in the fridge for 2 days before serving as an apéritif or liqueur.

COOK'S TIP
Try serving this over lots of ice in a tall tumbler for a deliciously long drink.

Tequila Cocktail

Tequila is distilled from the fermented sap of the blue agave plant and gets its name from the town of Tequila, where it has been made for more than 200 years. It is very strong, though brands destined for export are generally of a lower strength than those distilled for consumption in Mexico.

Serves 2

INGREDIENTS
100 ml/3¹/₂ fl oz/scant ¹/₂ cup
    white tequila
90 ml/6 tbsp freshly squeezed
    lime juice
30 ml/2 tbsp grenadine syrup
crushed ice
twists of lime rind, to serve

white tequila

lime juice

grenadine syrup

lime rind

1 Combine the tequila, lime juice and grenadine syrup in a mixing glass and stir to mix thoroughly.

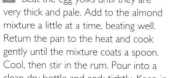

2 Three-quarters fill two cocktail glasses with crushed ice and carefully pour the tequila cocktail mixture into each glass. Serve each drink with one or two short drinking straws and a twist of lime rind.

COOK'S TIP
The traditional way to drink tequila is to place some salt on the back of the left hand between the base of the thumb and index finger. Taking care not to spill the salt, hold a halved lime in the same hand. Then hold a small tequila glass in the right hand. Lick a little salt, down the tequila and immediately suck the lime.

Bloody Maria

This variation on a classic Bloody Mary is made with tequila instead of vodka.

Serves 2

INGREDIENTS
175 ml/6 fl oz/³/₄ cup tomato juice
90 ml/6 tbsp white tequila
dash each of Worcestershire and
    Tabasco sauces
30 ml/2 tbsp lemon juice
salt and freshly ground black pepper
8 ice cubes

tomato juice

white tequila

Worcestershire sauce

Tabasco sauce

lemon juice

1 Combine the tomato juice, tequila, Worcestershire and Tabasco sauces and lemon juice in a cocktail shaker. Add salt and pepper to taste and four ice cubes. Shake very vigorously.

2 Place the remaining ice cubes in two heavy-based tumblers and strain the mixture over them.

COOK'S TIP
When drinks are to be served with ice, make sure all the ingredients are thoroughly chilled ahead of time.

Margarita

The Margarita is the most popular and well-known drink made with tequila. Freshly squeezed lime juice and salt are the traditional accompaniments to this fiery spirit, and are the other essential ingredients of this classic cocktail.

Serves 2

INGREDIENTS
¹/₂ lime
salt
120 ml/4 fl oz/¹/₂ cup white tequila
30 ml/2 tbsp Cointreau or Triple Sec
30 ml/2 tbsp freshly squeezed
    lime juice
4 or more ice cubes

lime   *salt*

           Cointreau

white tequila

1 Rub the rims of two cocktail glasses with the lime. Pour some salt into a saucer and dip in the glasses so that the rims are frosted.

2 Combine the tequila, Cointreau or Triple Sec and lime juice in a jug and stir to mix well. Pour the tequila mixture into the prepared glasses. Add the ice cubes and serve at once.

COOK'S TIP
To keep your Margaritas absolutely ice-cold, chill the glasses in the fridge, after salting the rims, until you are ready to fill them.

Chocolate Corn Drink

In Mexico, drinking chocolate is beaten with a very pretty carved wooden whisk called a *molinillo*, but a wire whisk does the job just as well.

Serves 6

INGREDIENTS
50 g/2 oz/scant ½ cup *masa harina* (tortilla flour)
750 ml/1¼ pints/3 cups water
5 cm/2 in cinnamon stick
750 ml/1¼ pints/3 cups milk
75 g/3 oz/3 squares Mexican chocolate or any unsweetened (bitter) chocolate, grated
a little soft light brown sugar

masa harina

cinnamon stick

milk   *chocolate*

brown sugar

I Combine the *masa harina* and water in a large saucepan, stirring to mix well. Add the cinnamon stick and cook, stirring, over a low heat until the mixture has thickened.

2 Gradually stir in the milk, then the grated chocolate. Continue to cook gently until all the chocolate has dissolved, beating with a whisk or a Mexican *molinillo*. Discard the cinnamon stick. Sweeten to taste with brown sugar. Serve hot in cups.

COOK'S TIP
If Mexican chocolate isn't available, use unsweetened (bitter) chocolate instead.

Mexican Hot Chocolate

Sweet dreams are guaranteed with this soothing Mexican speciality, whisked into a velvety froth and drunk very hot.

Serves 1

INGREDIENTS
250 ml/8 fl oz/1 cup milk or water or a mixture
40 g/1½ oz Mexican chocolate or any unsweetened (bitter) chocolate

milk

chocolate

I Put the milk or water in a saucepan with the chocolate and slowly bring to a simmer over a low heat. Simmer, stirring continuously, until the chocolate has melted. Continue to heat gently for 4–5 minutes to blend the flavours.

2 Pour the chocolate into a jug and beat with a Mexican *molinillo* until frothy. If a *molinillo* is not available, use a whisk or an electric mixer. Pour the chocolate into a mug and serve at once.

COOK'S TIP
Mexican cocoa beans are highly roasted to give a strong, bitter flavour, then coarsely ground with sugar and sometimes with cinnamon and vanilla. The chocolate is not milled between rollers to give the melt-in-the-mouth smoothness of European chocolate, but retains a characteristic gritty texture.

INDEX